CONTENTS

Cruel Crime
And
Painful Punishment

Terry Deary

Illustrated by
Mike Phillips

SCHOLASTIC

This book is dedicated to Michael MacDermid,
who is so addicted to *Horrible Histories* it's a crime.

Scholastic Children's Books,
Commonwealth House, 1–19 New Oxford Street,
London WC1A 1NU, UK

A division of Scholastic Ltd
London ~ New York ~ Toronto ~ Sydney ~ Auckland
Mexico City ~ New Delhi ~ Hong Kong

Published in the UK by Scholastic Ltd, 2002

Text copyright © Terry Deary, 2002
Cover illustration copyright © Martin Brown, 2002
Inside illustrations copyright © Mike Phillips, 2002

ISBN 0 439 97927 7

Typeset by M Rules
Printed by WS Bookwell, Finland

2 4 6 8 10 9 7 5 3 1

The right of Terry Deary, Martin Brown and Mike Phillips to be identified as
the author and illustrators of this work respectively has been asserted by
them in accordance with the Copyright, Designs and Patents Act, 1988.

INTRODUCTION

Everybody loves a good crime, don't they?

We can sit and watch it on our televisions for hours every night. Manglesome murderers, bold burglars, fiddling fraudsters and shocking shoplifters…

Then something happens…

…and suddenly we decide…

Then those bothersome burglars aren't so much fun. Then we want them a) caught and b) punished.

In history different people have had different ideas about punishments. Some people have been kind to killers and forgiving to forgers – other people have been savage to sweetie-snatchers and brutal to beggars. The aim of punishment is usually to stop the crime happening again...

SHE TALKED IN MY LESSON – CUT OUT HER TONGUE.

In the past few thousand years there have been a) some cruel crimes and some painful punishments and b) some kind crimes – and some pitiful punishments. This book is a *Horrible History* of crime and punishment. So guess which sort you are going to get in these pages?

(Guess wrong and you will be tied to a chair, bare-footed, and your toes will be nibbled off by flesh-eating ducks. Maybe.)

ANCIENT CRIME TIME

What was the first crime in time? Probably something to do with greed. You know the sort of thing...

(People are still snatching from the weak in the 21st century. Greed, and crimes of greed, don't change much, as you'll see.)

There must have been 'spoken' rules about how to behave as soon as humans could speak ... and most rules would have had a punishment.

Then humans invented 'writing' and they began writing down these rules and punishments as 'laws'.

These ancient groups of laws are often known as 'codes'. Here's a timeline of the most important ones...

Criminal codes timeline

4000 BC: BABYLON

A law says that speaking badly about a priest or a married woman will be punished by 'branding' (a mark is burned into the law-breaker's skin using a red-hot iron). Ouch!

2350 BC: URUKAGINA'S CODE

A set of laws is laid down by Mesopotamian kings. They are fairly harsh. Savage sample:

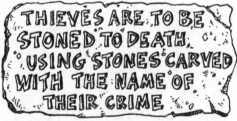

2050 BC: UR-NAMMU'S CODE

This Mesopotamian code lets judges decide 'damages' – where the criminal has to pay the victim. The worse the crime the more you pay...

1850 BC: THE EARLIEST-KNOWN LEGAL DECISION IS MADE.

A clay tablet tells of the murder of a temple-worker. Three men and the victim's wife were charged. Nine witnesses spoke against the men and woman and asked for the death penalty for all four.

But the wife had two witnesses who told the court that her dead husband used to beat her. What's more, they said, she was not part of the murder and she was even worse off after her husband's death.

What would you do if you were the judge?
a) execute the three men and the woman
b) execute the three men but not the woman
c) execute the woman but not the men

1700 BC: HAMMURABI'S CODE

King Hammurabi comes to power in Babylon in 1792 BC. In 1700 BC, his code of laws is carved on a huge rock column. The saying 'an eye for an eye and a tooth for a tooth' comes from Hammurabi's code. The code has 282 clauses and the punishments are, by modern western standards, barbaric. Savage sample:

THEFT - THE THIEF WILL LOSE A FINGER OR A HAND

What do you imagine was the punishment for kissing a married woman? Your lower lip was cut off!

YES! I KNOW I KISSED HER - AND I KNOW SHE'S A MARRIED WOMAN - BUT SHE'S MY MUM!

1300 BC: THE TEN COMMANDMENTS

The Bible says that Moses received a list of ten laws straight from God. These laws were known as the Ten Commandments. Most of these commandments are still part of our laws, like 'thou shalt not kill'. But there are no punishments for the crimes — except the anger of God, of course.

IF YOU STEAL THAT SHEEP I'LL BE A BIT CROSS WITH YOU... AND YOU WOULDN'T WANT THAT, WOULD YOU?

NO, GOD!

Of course human law-makers may need a bit more than anger to put criminals off...

IF YOU STEAL THAT SHEEP I'LL BE A BIT CROSS WITH YOU... AND YOU WOULDN'T WANT THAT, WOULD YOU?

NO, SIR!

NOT AGAIN!

1280 BC to 880 BC: THE LAWS OF MANU

In India, the great Laws of Manu are written down but no one knows exactly when or who wrote them. Savage sample:

> HE WHO RAISES HIS HAND OR A STICK, SHALL HAVE HIS HAND CUT OFF.
> HE WHO IN ANGER KICKS WITH HIS FOOT, SHALL HAVE HIS FOOT CUT OFF.

621 BC: DRACO'S LAW

Draco the Greek is chosen to write a code of law for Athens. His laws are the first written laws of Greece. The penalty for many offences is death. The citizens adore Draco and one day arrange a party for him. The loving people of Athens shower him with their hats and cloaks to show their love for the man. By the time they dig him out from under the clothes, he has been smothered to death.

THAT'S WHAT YOU GET FOR BEING POPULAR...

600 BC: LYCURGUS' LAW

This King of Sparta (southern Greece) becomes a famous law-maker, though his laws are never written down. Savage sample:

IT IS THE DUTY OF WOMEN TO HAVE CHILDREN. IF ANY CHILD IS NOT PERFECT WHEN BORN THEY ARE TO BE KILLED.

THE GREATEST CRIME OF ALL IS TO RETREAT IN BATTLE—PUNISHABLE BY DEATH.

536 BC: THE BOOK OF PUNISHMENTS

This Chinese law book lists the ways to punish someone when they have been convicted of a serious crime. They include:

I CAN TATTOO YOU, CUT OFF YOUR NOSE, OR YOUR FEET...OR YOUR HEAD...

OOOH! THINK I'LL GO FOR THE TATTOO, IF IT'S ALL THE SAME TO YOU.

450 BC: THE TWELVE TABLES

Ten Roman men are given power to write the laws that are to govern Romans. They come up with ten laws to which two were later added. Our modern laws are still based on this Roman top-twelve. But not ALL twelve, you'll be pleased to hear, because one of them said:

The Twelve Tables also punished the evil use of magic! They were written on wood and bronze sheets, and survived for almost 1000 years until they were destroyed by invading Gauls in 390.

399 BC: THE TRIAL OF SOCRATES

One of the earliest reported trials takes place in Greece. The city of Athens has lost a war and is looking for someone to blame. The people blame 70-year-old Socrates – a teacher accused of showing Athens boys bad ways and telling them not to believe in the gods.

Socrates is tried before a jury of 501 citizens that finds him 'guilty' on a vote of 281–220.

The judge then asks Socrates what would be a fair punishment. Socrates replies. . .

If Socrates had said something sensible, like 'Exile me!', then the jury would probably have given him a lesser punishment. But by calling the jury idiots he might as well have just killed himself. The jury decide 'Death' by 361 votes to 140. (Find out what happened to surly Soc later.)

Be warned! If someone is about to punish you, it is not wise to insult them. . .

11

Let the punishment fit the ancient crime

The tricky bit about crime and punishment is making the one match the other. People have different ideas about how you should punish a crime and these ideas have changed through time. Laws in ancient times seem a bit harsh to us today. The Bible says...

> Whoever curses his father or mother is to be put to death.

If that rule was in force today we'd have a lot of empty classrooms and a lot of empty schools. Death seems just a teeny bit harsh for cursing parents. What would *you* do if you were a parent?

WOULD YOU LIKE YOUR SON KILLED, SIR?

GOOD HEAVENS, NO. WE'RE NOT BARBARIANS. JUST STRETCH HIM ON THE RACK, PLEASE.

Fitting the right punishment to a crime has always been a problem. Can you match these ancient crimes and their punishments?

CRIME	PUNISHMENT
1 A Mesopotamian holy woman drinking in a pub	a) fifty lashes
2 A Babylonian son hitting his father	b) having your eye pulled out
3 A Mesopotamian rebelling against the king	c) being thrown off a cliff
4 An Egyptian taking a day off work	d) being bitten on the back of the hand
5 A Spartan child servant making a mistake	e) cutting off a hand
6 In the Bible, killing a burglar in the night	f) stoning to death
7 A Babylonian accusing an innocent person of a crime	g) having an ear cut off
8 In Babylon, a slave striking his master	h) burning
9 In the Bible, being a lazy son	i) being skinned alive
10 A Babylonian putting out someone's eye	j) no punishment

Answers:

1h) Imagine burning a nun because she popped in a pub for a pint!

2e) But fathers were allowed to hit sons. Life can be cruel to kids, can't it?

3i) King Ashurnasirpal skinned a lot of rebels and buried a lot of others alive inside a stone column. Then he had their crimes written on the column – which is how we know about them today.

4a) This was a punishment for weavers who made cloth. But it's not so long since children in Britain were beaten just for taking a day off from school.

5d) In the army training camps younger children served the older ones. If they got it wrong the older boy bit the younger boy's hand.

6j) Killing a burglar in your own home was not a crime – if you did it at night. But if you did it during the day it was murder and you'd be punished.

7c) Lying about an innocent person is called 'slander', and you can still be sent to prison for it – so watch what you say!

8g) There is no ear-chopping from people who strike masters today – otherwise there might be a lot of ear-less pupils in schools!

9f) The Bible says: "If a man has a stubborn and rebellious son, who will not obey the voice of his father or the voice of his mother, then his father and his mother shall take hold of him and bring him to the elders of his city. Then all the men of the city shall stone him to death with stones."

10b) This idea is known as 'an eye for an eye'. Some people still believe this is a good way to match crimes and punishments.

How did you score?

10 You were probably cheating. Punishment: cut your toenails.

5–9 Not bad. Punishment: write out the correct answers 50 times.

1–4 Pathetic. Punishment: write out the correct answers 1,000 times.

0 Serious failure. Punishment: cut off your head and replace it with one with brains.

Did you know…?

It was a crime in Ancient Britain to be old and helpless. The rest of your tribe could not be expected to work to feed you. So, when you became feeble (about the age of 32) you were expected to throw yourself off a cliff. If you didn't, then the tribe would just chuck you off.

HAPPY BIRTHDAY TO YOU...
HAPPY BIRTHDAY TO YOU...

THANKS!

Groovy Greeks

The Greeks had some interesting ways of dealing with their criminals. But can you sort out who got what? Sadly our *Horrible Histories* law book has been cut up by some cunning criminal. Can you replace the words in their right places?

1 LIVING IN A CITY LIKE ATHENS IS THE BEST WAY OF LIFE SO IT IS AN AWFUL PUNISHMENT TO BE _____.

2 A GREEK MAN MUST NOT STRIKE ANOTHER GREEK MAN OR WOMAN. IF HE DOES HE WILL BE _____.

3 A SLAVE WILL BE _____ IF HE THREATENS SOMEONE WITH IRON, WOOD OR BRONZE.

4 GOOD PEOPLE OF ATHENS BELIEVE IN THE OLD GODS. A MAN WHO TEACHES YOUNG PEOPLE NOT TO BELIEVE IN THE GODS WILL BE _____.

5 ATHENS LORD DRACO ORDERS THAT IF YOU OWE MONEY YOU COULD BE _____.

6 A WOMAN CAUGHT SNEAKING IN TO THE OLYMPIC GAMES WILL BE _____.

7 DRACO SAYS THAT ANYONE STEALING SHOULD BE _____.

8 LEADERS WHO BETRAY SPARTA CAN EXPECT TO BE _____.

MISSING WORDS: ENSLAVED, POISONED, EXECUTED, ASSASSINATED, FINED, THROWN OFF A CLIFF, BANISHED, LASHED

Answers:

1 Banished. Inside the city of Athens you were protected by walls, by laws *and* by the goddess Athena. Men of Athens could scratch the name of someone they wanted thrown out on a piece of pottery and pop it in a voting box. The name that appeared most was sent out of the city. (Good idea for school bullies?)

2 Fined. How much would you fine fighting fellers? A pound a punch? A penny a pinch? A fiver a fisting? A tenner a trampling?

3 Lashed. The punishment was a hundred lashes – which is a lot.

4 Poisoned. Teacher Socrates taught the youths of Athens not to believe in the old gods so he was told to drink poison – hemlock – which he did. This is not too bad a punishment – a lot of teachers today would rather drink poison than teach today's savage students and poisonous pupils. (Or so they say after a bad day with 7F.)

5 Enslaved. If you owed a man money then you could become that man's slave till it was paid.

6 Thrown off a cliff. Women weren't welcome at the games, where the men all ran and jumped and threw and wrestled with no clothes on. One woman was a trainer and tried to sneak in. She was killed.

7 Executed. Deadly Draco also said you'd be executed for stealing an apple or a cabbage. And anyone who was lazy could be executed too.

8 Assassinated. Athenian general, Alcibiades, switched sides from Athens to Sparta. He then helped Sparta to win a war against the Athenians. But the Spartans didn't trust him and they set fire to his house. As he ran out of the blazing building they filled him full of arrows.

GUESS I DIDN'T HAVE AN ARROW ESCAPE THIS TIME!

Rotten Romans

The Romans were famous for making laws. It is said that Roman law was the start of most of the laws we still have today. But that doesn't mean the Roman laws were fair or free of cruelty. They weren't! One way of executing a criminal was especially nasty…

Of course you should never do this, not even to your worst enemy. It absolutely ruins the barrel.

So, if anyone tries to tell you the Romans had 'modern' laws, just remind them that it was the Romans who liked to nail criminals to crosses. That wasn't as quick as throwing them to lions to be ripped apart, but the crosses could be put up at the side of the main roads so travellers could see the criminals slowly dying.

Of course the most famous victim of this punishment was Jesus. And his followers suffered just as much at the hands of the rotten Romans…

Cruel for Christians

Being a Christian has often been a 'crime' in history. But it was the Emperor Nero who really had it in for the Christians.

In AD 64 there was a huge fire that destroyed a large area of Rome. The Romans were angry and looking for someone to blame. They decided to blame their emperor – Nero – even though he wasn't in Rome at the time. They said he started the fire to clear away a large area of houses so he could build a palace.

Nero needed to find someone else to blame – and he chose a group of Jews who followed the teachings of Jesus: the Christians. He started executing them and the Romans enjoyed the idea. They even came up with new excuses for killing Christians who ate bread and drank wine, saying it was the flesh and blood of Jesus…

And they did. The Roman historian Tacitus wrote:

History of Rome by Tacitus

Book 15, AD 62–65

Mockery of every sort was added to their deaths. They were covered with the skins of wild beasts, and then they were torn to death by dogs, or were nailed to crosses, or were thrown to the flames and burnt, to serve as flaming torches when darkness fell.

Nero offered his gardens for the executions, and was putting on a show in the circus, while he mixed with the people in the dress of a chariot driver.

But the people were not fooled and even for criminals who deserved punishment, there arose a feeling of pity. The Romans knew the executions were not for the good of Rome, they were for the pleasure of one cruel man, Emperor Nero.

Even though Nero died four years after the fire, the execution of Christians went on without him and the methods were just as cruel.

Poetic passions

Some of the descriptions of Christians thrown to the lions come from Christians themselves. They didn't just hate the death of their friends – they hated the pleasure the Romans got from watching the bloody deaths. One Christian wrote a poem…

AT THE COLOSSEUM
by Amphilochius of Iconium

They watch and don't care in the least
As one poor man runs from the beast.

He's caught, just hear the claps and cheers;
Their eyes are filled with joy, not tears.

They show no pity in their looks
As victims' blood flows like a brook.

They scream for more such human feasts
And grind their teeth like hungry beasts.

Criminal cuts

The Romans didn't just enjoy watching Christians slaughtered in the 'games'. Ordinary criminals were killed too. (Usually around lunchtime.)

Some of the bloodiest battles in the 'games' were between criminals who were under sentence of death anyway. They fought till there was no one left…

• An unarmed man was put in the ring with an armed man who killed him. The armed man was then disarmed and the next man killed *him*.

- And so it went on – as soon as one victim fell another was put in the ring.
- Just to make sure the criminal was dead a slave would smash the fallen man over the head with a hammer.

Being a spectator had its dangers too. One spectator made a joke about the emperor, Domitian. He was taken out of the crowd and thrown to a pack of dogs!

Ripped rebel

The historian Strabo described a special 'entertainment' that the Romans saved for a rebel leader…

A rebel called Selurus had put himself at the head of an army and for a long time had raided the people of Etna. I saw him torn to pieces by wild beasts at a games event in the Forum. He was put on to a tall tower, a bit like Mount Etna where he had raided. The model mountain suddenly broke up and collapsed. Selurus tumbled down with it into cages of wild beasts that had been set up beneath the model.

Cheating the law

The Romans had special serving women in a temple called the Temple of Vesta. They were known as the 'Vestal Virgins'. These ladies had to behave themselves or they would be executed. The trouble is, you couldn't lay a finger on the Vestal Virgins – they were servants of the gods, who might get angry.

So how do you get rid of Vestal Virgins who misbehaved?

Answer:
They were buried alive. They were sent down into an underground room which was blocked up, and left to suffocate or starve to death. Nice.

Deading Dad

Romans who killed their father had a special punishment:

1 The executioner took a large sack and placed a dog, a cockerel and a monkey in it.
2 Then he put the dad-killing criminal in the sack.
3 Then sewed up the sack.
4 And threw it into the River Tiber.

Of course the dad-killer died – but so did the dog, the monkey and the cockerel! What had *they* done to deserve it?

Roman army rules

Punishments for soldiers who commit crimes have often been much harder than for other criminals. Soldiers have to learn that there is something *worse* than the terrifying enemy ... the punishment they'll get from their *own* army if they try to run away or disobey the rules! In the Roman army...

- If you did something that put your unit in danger then you'd be stoned to death ... and your unit would throw the stones!
- If you ran away from a battle you'd suffer death by beating.
- If your whole unit ran away from a battle, and was caught, then one man in ten would be executed. The soldiers would draw lots to decide who the lucky (and unlucky!) ones were.

DO I WIN A PRIZE IF I GET IT RIGHT?

Mangling Manu

In India around AD 100 there were the Laws of Manu. The laws were linked to your 'caste' or level in society – and so were the punishments. Peasants (lower 'castes') had different laws from the rich people and the lords of India (the higher 'castes').

The Brahmin caste (the priests) had it easiest. The Warrior caste were punished more, the farmer caste more still and the slave caste most of all.

Here's a list of mangling Manu crimes and punishments – which of these laws are true and which are false?

1 You can't be a witness in court if you are drunk.

2 Any child who sticks out a tongue at a teacher will have that tongue cut out.

3 If someone in a lower caste spits on someone in a higher caste then he shall have his lips cut off.

4 Any child who forgets to do homework will have to clean the school toilets.

5 If you attack someone, and hurt them, then you have to pay for a doctor to cure them.

6 Any child who doesn't eat their school dinner will have it pushed up their nose.

7 Anyone who grabs the king's hair will have his hands cut off.

8 Any girl who grabs a boy's hair will have her hair cut off.

Answers:
1, 3, 5, 7 are true. And, by the way, you couldn't be a witness in court if you were mad, tired or hungry either.

DREADFUL DARK AGES

The Dark Ages (around AD 400–1000) are sometimes thought of as 'lawless'. When the Romans left Britain, the Angles and Saxons invaded. Then the Vikings began to rampage around Europe murdering monks, flattening farmers, bashing babies and terrorizing towns. But the deadly Dark Ages did have their own methods of punishment...

Artful Alfred

King Alfred ruled Britain from 871 till 901. He took all the old laws and organized them into a new book of laws for the Saxons.

There were ways of finding out if a person was guilty of a crime. They were called 'ordeals'. If you passed through the ordeal you were innocent – but if you failed you were guilty ... and you suffered from both the test and then a punishment.

1 Ordeal by cake

A special cake is baked. The victim has to swear, 'If I did this crime then may this cake choke me!' and eat the cake. Sounds harmless enough, but Earl Godwin was banished from England for disobeying the good King Edward – a year later Godwin returned and declared...

A minute later Godwin was dead. He had choked on the piece of bread!

2 Ordeal by cold water

The accused is tied hand and foot. A rope is placed around them and they are lowered into a pool. If they sink then they are innocent ... and if they

float then they are guilty. (This test was still being used in the 17th century to test people accused of being witches! More about that later…)

3 Ordeal by hot water

The accused must plunge a bare arm into a pot of hot water and pull out a stone at the bottom of the pot. The arm will then be bandaged for three days. At the end of three days the bandage will be taken off. If the arm is healed then they are innocent … but, if there is still a scald, they are guilty and must be punished.

4 Ordeal by hot metal

The accused must grip a hot iron rod and walk with it for a set distance. Again the hand is bandaged for three days and the wound examined.

5 Ordeal by lot

Try this in your own classroom!

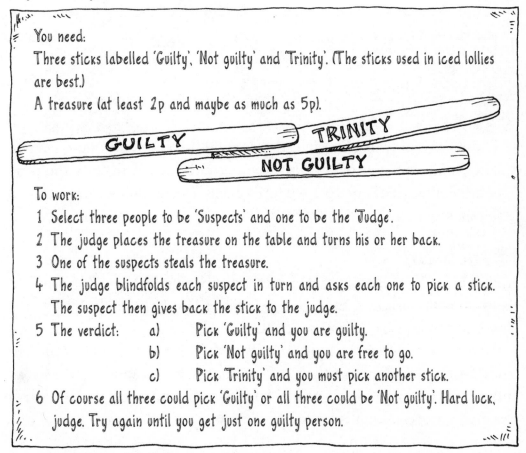

You need:
Three sticks labelled 'Guilty', 'Not guilty' and 'Trinity'. (The sticks used in iced lollies are best.)
A treasure (at least 2p and maybe as much as 5p).

GUILTY   TRINITY   NOT GUILTY

To work:
1 Select three people to be 'Suspects' and one to be the 'Judge'.
2 The judge places the treasure on the table and turns his or her back.
3 One of the suspects steals the treasure.
4 The judge blindfolds each suspect in turn and asks each one to pick a stick. The suspect then gives back the stick to the judge.
5 The verdict: a)   Pick 'Guilty' and you are guilty.
             b)   Pick 'Not guilty' and you are free to go.
             c)   Pick 'Trinity' and you must pick another stick.
6 Of course all three could pick 'Guilty' or all three could be 'Not guilty'. Hard luck, judge. Try again until you get just one guilty person.

Try it. Does it work? It's not as painful as trial by boiling water but you could be found guilty just by picking the wrong stick. Good idea for football matches though – better than a penalty shoot-out.

6 Ordeal by combat

If two people argue about who owns a brooch or a piece of land (or a stale cheese sandwich) then they have a fight. The winner of the fight is judged to be the lawful owner. Actually, this still goes on in schools today!

Saxon sentences

Alfred gave his judges a clear idea of what punishments to give for crimes:

- The penalty for killing a man accidentally by letting a tree fall on him was to be forced to give the tree to the family of the dead man.

- The penalty for telling lies about a person was to have your tongue cut out.
- The penalty for murder was to pay a fine to the relatives of the dead person. The payment to a victim's relatives was known as wer-gild (blood money).

French fines

Alfred brought these payments into English law but he didn't invent them. Across Europe at that time there were similar laws. In France the laws told judges exactly how much to fine a killer.

Payment was often 'in kind' not in cash. The values were roughly: a healthy ox = 2 solidi, a stallion = 7 solidi, a mare = 3 solidi, and a sword and scabbard = 7 solidi. A 'solidi' was the value of a cow. So 100 solidi was a very large amount of money.

Got the idea? Now match the fines to the crimes…

Answers:

1d) You could probably get an untrained slave – or a History teacher – for about half that.

2a) A boy under 12 was also worth 600. They were expensive to kill because it was thought they couldn't protect themselves – the law 'protected' them with a high wer-gild.

3e) If a corpse was hidden or dumped down a well then the fine was three times as great. A warrior was worth 600 solidi, but a warrior dumped down a well was worth 1,800 solidi. As you probably know, your dad's cash machine only lets him take out about £300 at a time. If Saxons had had cow machines they wouldn't have let you draw out 1,800 cows in one go.

4b) A free man was worth just 200 solidi. But if he was dumped down a well or hidden under branches he was worth three times that sum. Just imagine you're a free man's wife: you came home one night and find him dead…

5c) Romans always cost a bit more than a normal free man. So, if you find yourself driving a car down a street in Rome one day, try not to knock over a local man – or else make sure you have 300 cows handy in the back seat in case you do.

Not so fine

Not everyone was happy with the idea of being paid for a dead relative. There's a charming story from France about a boy called Chrammesind that shows that laws don't always keep people happy…

Once upon a time there was a boy called Chrammesind who lived in a great castle with his family. The family were poor – it costs a lot to keep a castle – and Chrammesind's clothes were ragged and threadbare.

One day the castle was attacked by a savage soldier called Sichar and everyone was killed – everyone except Chrammesind.

Sichar saw Chrammesind and liked the lad a lot. 'I'm not really such a bad chap,' Sichar said.

'You killed my family,' Chrammesind reminded him.

'Only because I wanted this castle,' Sichar told the boy. 'Nothing personal.'

'Oh, that's all right then,' Chrammesind said.

And so the two became friends and hunted and ate together. One evening, as it was growing dark, Sichar drank a goblet of wine and started to boast to his young friend Chrammesind. 'You were poor before I came!'

'I was,' the boy admitted.

'Now you have the wer-gild I paid for your family,' the savage Sichar smirked. 'I have filled your castle with gold and silver.'

'You have,' Chrammesind agreed.

'And you have all the castle. I did you a favour when I killed your kindred!'

Chrammesind sighed. 'But if I don't take revenge on my dead family everyone will say I am as weak as a woman.'

With that he blew out the candle, took his axe and hacked Sichar's skull in two.

THE END

Horrible history crime tale. BUT … there's one odd thing about it. Why did Chrammesind blow out the candle before he axed Sichar? So Sichar couldn't see what he was doing? But if Sichar couldn't see his axe then Chrammesind couldn't see Sichar's skull, could he? Very odd.

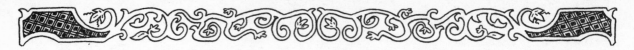

MURDEROUS MIDDLE AGES

How do you get someone you suspect of committing a crime to tell you the truth? Hurt them. Then tell them you'll keep on hurting them till they tell you everything you want to know. This is torture. Sometimes it is used to get a criminal's friends to betray them. You know the sort of thing…

I WANT TO KNOW WHO PUT THIS DRAWING PIN ON MY CHAIR. UNTIL YOU TELL ME THE WHOLE CLASS WILL STAY BEHIND AFTER SCHOOL.

Some people suffer torture well…

YOU CAN KEEP ME IN FOR EVER BUT I'LL NEVER TELL YOU IT WAS SARAH SLAPCHOP WOT DUN IT!

Over the years torture has been used to get criminals to confess.

YOU DID IT, SARAH SLAPCHOP. ADMIT IT OR I'LL KEEP YOU AN HOUR AFTER SCHOOL EVERY DAY UNTIL YOU DO.

DON'T CARE. WASN'T ME.

Not all tortures are about pain. Some are about driving you out of your mind. Someone can confess after a spell of 'solitary confinement' (locked up alone) or of 'sensory deprivation' (locked in a dark, silent cell with nothing to do).

TWO WEEKS LATER

TUCK SHOP

NYAAAAGH! IT WAS ME! I ADMIT IT! LET ME OUT!

THUMP! THUMP!

History

Some of the most terrible torturers of all time were churchmen in the Middle Ages…

Evil Inquisition

In the Middle Ages, the Christian Church became very worried. Some churchmen believed that some Christians were changing sides and following the Devil – also known as Satan, Beelzebub, the Evil One, the Prince of Darkness, Lucifer … or Old Nick as his mates in Hell call him.

So how do you get someone to own up and say, 'Yes, I worship the Devil'? Well, you torture them until they admit it and then you can burn them.

The bit of the Catholic Church that put people on trial was known as 'the Inquisition'. The Inquisition 'found' thousands of Devil worshippers. And they used some pretty cruel tricks to get people to talk…

Pope Innocent IV said that victims should *not* lose a limb or their life. So the Inquisition usually crushed fingers and toes, hands and feet, legs and arms…

- The torturers used nasty little things called 'thumbscrews' to squeeze down on fingernails.
- Red-hot pincers would be used to nip at the skin or the victims were simply roasted over hot coals.
- Sometimes the victims would be hung up with a rope around the wrists while weights were added to the feet.
- Water was poured into their mouths till the victims felt they were drowning.

Pope Clement V tried to cut back on the terrible tortures by saying:

So what did the torturers do? They tortured the victims day and night till they confessed.

Of course, most people will say *anything* if you torture them enough. In 1637, a woman was arrested at Eichstatt in Germany and put on trial…

THE WOMAN LAUGHED OUT LOUD WHEN TOLD SHE WAS A DEVIL WORSHIPPER…

I'D RATHER DIE THAN DO SUCH A THING. I'VE LED A LAWFUL LIFE FOR TWENTY YEARS WITH MY HUSBAND AND EIGHT CHILDREN.

THREE WEEKS LATER SHE DIED UNDER TORTURE. HER LAST WORDS WERE…

I AM IN LOVE WITH THE DEVIL, I KILLED A FRIEND'S BABY BECAUSE THE DEVIL TOLD ME TO… AND 45 OF MY NEIGHBOURS WORSHIP SATAN AS WELL!

> *Did you know…?*
> The Inquisition said children under 10 didn't have to be questioned and then tortured – they could just be tortured straight away. (Torturing and questioning children still goes on in Britain today where it is called SAT testing.)

Painless tortures

You may think torture means pain – but it doesn't always! Here are some that are really quite painless…

The Chinese water torture

This torture wasn't painful at all! The prisoner was tied to a table and his head was strapped in place so that he couldn't move anything … but his eyes. Water was then dripped on to his forehead, one drop at a time.

Eventually, this drove you crazy, they say. So after a while the victim would tell the secret, confess to the crime, or agree to do anything to get them to stop the drip, drip, drip. This was a useful torture when the torturers didn't want to show any marks on the victim, so they could say…

TORTURE? WE NEVER TOUCHED HIM!

This is a famous torture – but some historians say it never happened! They say it was made up by Americans who hated the Chinese and wanted to make them look evil.

The ghastly goat torture

Do you suspect your next-door neighbour of throwing a bucket of water over your cat while it was singing in his garden last night? Will nasty neighbour own up? No? Then torture him with this medieval French torture...

You need:
Stocks
A bucket of salt water
A goat

To torture:

1 Build or borrow a set of stocks – two planks with holes for the feet that hold the victim in place.

2 Remove victim's socks and place their feet in the stocks – if they are nervous tell them you want to give their toenails a trim.

3 Pour salt water over the victim's feet – if it's cold on a freezing day then all the better.

4 Show the goat the feet – goats adore salt and will use their very rough tongue to lick the feet of the victim.

5 The victim will probably confess after two seconds of this terrible tickling. If they don't then pour on more salt water and repeat.

It seems this torture really worked for the French.

Did you know...?

In 1975, the United Nations made a declaration against torture: 'No state may permit torture or other cruel punishment.' Yet, in the 1990s, there were still no laws against using torture in 60 countries.

Horrible habits

In Europe during the Middle Ages new punishments were invented to replace the old Saxon ones. They were supposed to be less cruel, but check this lot out…

The ducking stool

Women who nagged their husbands too much or who were caught fighting in the street would be sentenced to the ducking stool. Tied to a chair on the end of a plank and dunked in the cold river a few times. This sometimes stopped the nagging for ever … careless duckers could accidentally drown their victims! Ducking stools were also used in Germany for bakers who sold bad bread or children who stole apples!

Stocks

For small offences the criminal would be placed in stocks. Their crime would be written on the board that held their legs and the public could add to the punishment by throwing things at the criminal. A market trader who cheated customers might get this treatment.

Pressing

If a prisoner refused to plea either guilty or not guilty then the jailers would lay them on the ground and put weights on them. Then they would 'press' them. They would stay there without food and water until they talked – or until they died. It later became a method of execution. (Margaret Clitheroe was sentenced to death by crushing in York in 1586. She refused to talk when questioned about hiding a Catholic priest. But no one actually wanted to splatter her, and two beggars had to be paid to do the dirty work.)

Pillory

The head and hands were held in a wooden frame and the victim had to stand. If they got tired and their bodies sagged – then the neck-hole could choke them. An old Newcastle woman almost died this way in 1758 – her crime was *fortune-telling*. In 1560 a London maid who tried to poison her mistress was placed in the pillory and had her ears cut off! Sometimes thousands of people gathered at the pillory – pickpockets had a wonderful time!

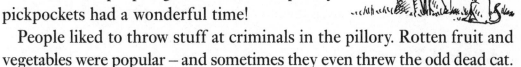

People liked to throw stuff at criminals in the pillory. Rotten fruit and vegetables were popular – and sometimes they even threw the odd dead cat.

The stocks and pillory were banned in the UK after 1837.

Did you know…?

In the Middle Ages the jailers of Venice, Italy, invented a collar with a bell attached. Like a cow-bell it helped the jailer to keep track of the prisoner. They could even leave the jail wearing it. It sounds harmless enough … but the non-stop jangling of the bell drove some prisoners mad!

Jailers in the 21st century don't use bells – they use 'electronic tags' instead. The local police can let a criminal out of jail but keep track of him with a radio signal sent from a band on his ankle. Police in England in 1999 made one slight mistake – they put a tag on a criminal's false leg. He just unfastened the leg – and *hopped it*!

VICIOUS VILLAINS

Some people can be really nasty. They don't rob and kill because they are poor or desperate – they do it purely for pleasure. They are real villains. Here are some people you would *not* want to meet on a dark night on a lonely mountain with only a piece of chewing gum for defence…

I Khan if I want to

Genghis Khan probably ruled a larger area than any other man or woman in history. He ruled Mongolia from 1206 to 1227 and sent his Mongol armies to conquer everyone in sight. Of course, you don't get that sort of power by being a cuddly koala bear, do you? No, Genghis was not the sort of chap you'd invite home for tea…

Grisly Genghis claimed he knew the secret of happiness – invading a foreign country and robbing it. He said…

> *The greatest happiness is to beat your enemies, to chase them in front of you, to rob them of their wealth, to see their loved ones bathed in tears, to steal their wives and daughters.*

The wives and daughters probably didn't see this as 'the greatest happiness'. But when you are a powerful ruler you can break laws and get away with it.

Genghis would tell you he was hard but fair. He killed a thief who stole from one of his tribe. So what? So, the thief was his own brother. Would you kill your own brother? Better not answer that.

Genghis had the 'Yassa' written – his own law book. Some of the laws in it aren't too surprising…

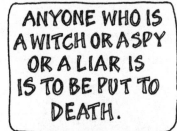 

ANYONE WHO IS A WITCH OR A SPY OR A LIAR IS IS TO BE PUT TO DEATH.

FAIR ENOUGH

But some of the Yassa laws would result in nearly EVERY single person in Britain being executed today! The Yassa said…

ANYONE WHO URINATES IN WATER IS TO BE PUT TO DEATH.

I WAS BURSTING!

On the Mongolian Plains water was as precious as gold – so anyone having a pee in the stuff would get the chop.

Tough? Yes, but it was said that the Yassa worked so well that carloads of gold could be left out untouched by the people.

Old Man of Masyad

You think your school's bad? You should have gone to the school run by the Old Man of Masyad – he taught his pupils how to die!

The Old Man was head of the Assassins in 1100 – a Middle Eastern group of people who believed they'd go straight to Heaven if they died fighting for their religion. An old script described his teaching…

The Old Man of Masyad brings up a large number of noble boys in his palace. They are taught every kind of subject and all languages so that they can talk in any country. Cruelty of the greatest degree is also taught. When they reach fourteen, the head teacher calls them to him and orders them to slay some great man, whom he names; and for this purpose he gives to each of them a dagger of terrible length and

sharpness. They never hesitate, nor do they pause until they have reached the prince who has been pointed out to them. They serve that prince until they find a chance to murder him – even if they die themselves. They believe that by doing so they shall win the favour of their god.

IT'S GREAT TO RELAX WITH YOUR MATES.

Today, people who kill leaders are still named 'assassins'. They don't see their murder as a crime – and some don't mind dying, so punishment doesn't stop them.

Balthasar Gerard

One of the strangest assassinations was that of Dutch ruler William of Orange in 1584. His killer, Balthasar Gerard, played the usual assassin trick and made friends with his target, who was also known as William the Silent. William trusted Balthasar Gerard and asked him to take a message to France...

BALTHASAR DIDN'T LEAVE THE PALACE...

WHY HAVEN'T YOU GONE YET?

YOUR MAJESTY, I HAVE NO MONEY FOR THE CLOTHES AND SHOES I NEED.

HERE'S A PURSE OF GOLD.

YOUR MAJESTY IS VERY KIND.

AND VERY, VERY STUPID.

CHINK! CHINK!

BALTHASAR WENT STRAIGHT TO A GUARD...

SELL ME YOUR PISTOLS!

I COULD USE THE MONEY.

And that's how William the Silent was silenced. It's a bit cruel, using someone's money to kill them. But it's not as cruel as what they did to Balthasar, who was publicly executed four days later. His flesh was torn from his body with red-hot pincers before his guts were pulled out and his body hacked into quarters. (By the way, the guard who sold the pistols killed himself too.)

Rotten Reginald of Kerak

Reggie was a Christian Crusader – his mission was to capture Jerusalem from the Muslims *and* make himself as rich as possible. The Muslims worshipped the prophet Mohammed and their greatest joy was to visit his grave. Rotten Reg had a revolting idea – he decided to steal the body of Mohammed and charge the Muslims to go and see it!

Reg failed, but only just. The leader of the Muslim warriors at that time was Saladin, who vowed, 'I will kill Reginald with my own hands!'

Then, in 1187 the Crusaders lost the Battle of Hattin. After the battle, Saladin gathered King Guy (of Jerusalem) and his leading knights (including Reginald) in his tent. Saladin told Reggie what he thought of him and then Reggie made a big mistake. He shrugged and said, 'I'm only doing what every Crusader does!'

Furious Saladin killed him with one blow of his sword.

Did you know...?

In Prague in 1398, Emperor Wenceslas had a cook who failed to provide a good meal. Wicked Wenceslas had the cook roasted over his own fire. He also went out hunting and shot a monk in the forest. His excuse was:

IT WAS HIS OWN FAULT. MONKS SHOULDN'T GO WANDERING IN THE FOREST!

Stick 'em up, Dracula!

In 1897 Bram Stoker wrote a book called *Dracula* and it soon became one of the most popular horror stories of all time. But where did Bram get the idea from? Meet two real-life vicious villains...

1 The real Dracula

HOW D'YOU LIKE YOUR STAKE?

There really was a cruel Count Vlad Dracula who ruled in Wallachia (part of modern Romania) in the 15th century. He was also known as Vlad the Impaler because his favourite nastiness was 'impaling' prisoners of war. What is impaling? You don't want to know! You do? Oh, well.

The victim was speared with a wooden spike, which was planted in the ground, and left to die a horrible and painful slow death. The impaling was often done through the stomach or the chest. But sometimes, for a change, Vlad would impale people upside-down through the skull.

KEBAB?

Vlad often had feasts where the victims were impaled around the walls of his dining hall. Nasty man. But just as nasty was...

2 Countess Elizabeth Bathory

This sad woman was known as 'The Blood Countess of Transylvania' (which is also a part of Romania in case you're looking for somewhere cheerful to spend your next holiday). Bloody Bess was born in 1560 into one of the richest families in Transylvania. She should have had a happy life – but she killed over 600 women and girls in the early 1600s. Why?

a) So she could have a bath in their blood.

b) So she could drink their blood.

c) Because she was jealous of their good looks.

Answer:

a) She bathed in blood to stay young. Bloodthirsty Bess had horrible henchmen to help her. They drained the blood from the victims and filled the baths. But one of her victims escaped and told the law officers about what was happening at Castle Csejthe. On 30 December 1610 they raided the castle. They were horrified by the terrible sights they found – one dead girl in the main room, drained of blood, and another alive whose body had been pierced with holes. In the dungeon they discovered several living girls, some of whose bodies had been pierced.

Bad Bess never actually went on trial and so she was never officially found guilty. And of course, being a countess, she had lots of powerful friends who tried to cover up her dreadful deeds. Her henchmen were executed – beheaded and burned after having their fingers torn out – but bad Bess was allowed to live, though she was put well out of harm's way. Stonemasons were brought to Castle Csejthe to brick up the windows and doors of the bedroom with the Countess inside. They left a small hole through which food could be passed. She stayed there for the rest of her life and died in the castle in 1614.

So there you have it – *two* real-life blood-lovers helped to give Bram his brainwave. Neither actually drank blood, though, and neither flitted around like a bat – but both were pretty batty.

Bernabo Visconti

Brutal Bernie ruled in Milan, Italy, around 1350. He had a fearful temper and often got angry as a giraffe with a sore throat. And when he rode down the streets of Milan everyone had to fall to their knees and bow as he passed – or else.

Bernabo's crimes...

- Bernabo wrote a list of punishments for anyone caught betraying him, and these included gouged eyes, sliced noses, hacked-off arms and legs 'one by one', as well as stretching on the rack and skinning alive.

- Bernabo's older brother was wasting the family fortune – Bernie had him murdered 'like a dog'.
- Bernabo argued with the Pope – he even raised an army and fought him.
- Bernabo believed nuns and monks were the Pope's spies – he had four nuns burned alive and had one captured monk placed in an iron cage over a fire and roasted alive.

- Bernabo received a letter from the Pope that upset him – so he forced the messenger to eat not only the letter, but the silk ribbon and the lead seals too.
- Bernabo was a keen huntsman with 500 dogs and if a dog ever fell sick he had the dog-keeper hanged.

- Bernabo's town suffered from the plague so Bernabo had all sick people carried out to the fields to die there.

Bernabo's punishment...

When Bernie was 76 he was sure people were out to kill him so he doubled his guard and had his food tasted for poison. Then one day his nephew, Gian, asked to meet him outside the city.

'It's a plot!' Bernabo's friends said.

Bernabo replied, 'You are stupid. I tell you, I know my nephew.'

He rode out with just two guards to meet Gian – who had a small army! Gian hugged Uncle Bernie before calling his men to cut off his sword belt and arrest him.

Bernie was locked away and left to die – except he wouldn't die quickly, so Gian had him poisoned.

Nasty people – nasty ending.

Awful for animals

Many animals have been brought to trial and punished for their crimes. The Bible says…

> If an ox gore a man or a woman so that they die, then the ox shall surely be stoned.

And through the years many animals have died for human laws they didn't know they'd broken…

- In the year 864, a hive of bees which stung a man to death was condemned to be exterminated.

- In Ansbach, in 1685, a wolf that had terrorized a village was killed. But it was first dressed in human clothes and hanged as an example to other wolves!

- In the 1700s, body-snatchers roamed the graveyards hoping to dig up your aunty Gladys's fresh corpse to sell it.

Worried families often tried to defend their dead relatives against body-snatchers. One way was to guard the graveyard every night – or pay someone to guard it for you. This was not a very pleasant job. One nervous guard armed himself with a pistol. He saw a pale shape moving behind a tree, thought it was an illegal trespasser and fired. When morning came he examined his victim … and found he had shot a pig!

- In France, in 1740, a cow was found guilty of witchcraft. It was hanged.
- A Swiss dog was charged, along with two men, of murder in 1906 – the men got life imprisonment but the dog was condemned to death.
- Even in 1974, in Italy, a dog that bit a man was sentenced to a month in prison on a diet of bread and water – it served the sentence and was released.
- Hens lay eggs – cockerels don't. So, when a cockerel was found sitting on an egg in medieval France it was accused of being a devil. It was burnt at the stake – and the executioner probably had a lovely roast chicken dinner.
- Animal trials are still going on. In 1992 an Indian newspaper announced…

An elephant which trampled a drunken attacker to death in Delhi, India, was arrested and put on trial in chains.

Did you know…?
A US cat-lover, Governor Pinchot, sentenced a dog to life imprisonment for killing his cat. The dog served six years in prison.

TORTURING
TUDORS

King Henry VIII ruled England from 1509 till 1547. The death sentence was used more in his reign than at any time in English history. About 72,000 people died for their crimes in his reign. (He even had two of his wives beheaded.)

Henry wanted power over everything and everyone. He even wanted power over the Church – so he got rid of the Catholic Church (whose head was the Pope) and made himself head of the Church of England. Henry killed or tortured anyone who opposed it.

For the rest of the century, Protestants and Catholics killed and tortured one another with ever-increasing cruelty. Here are some of the terrible Tudor methods…

Amputation

Fighting in a royal palace had been a crime before Henry's time. Any fight could lead to the monarch being injured. The fighter would be executed. Henry wasn't so harsh. He punished this crime by ruling that…

Branding

It was difficult to keep criminal records in Tudor times – there were no computers and no photographs. So, to keep a check on a criminal's offences, they were recorded on the criminals themselves!

A letter was burned into the flesh of the hand or wrist. Henry made these 'brands' standard across the country. Some letters were…

Did you know…?

A prisoner could cheat this punishment. If they could afford 13 pence then the branding iron would be *cold* when it was pressed on to the skin!

Burning at the stake

Henry's daughter, Mary, was a Catholic. When she came to the throne in 1553 she began to burn Protestants at the stake. Catholics like Mary believed that fire would burn away all evil so the purified souls could then go straight to heaven. They were doing their victims a *favour* by burning them! They looked to the Bible which said:

> The angels shall gather all things that offend and shall cast them into a furnace of fire.

They must be Hell's Angels.

To make death quicker and kinder the victims had pouches of gunpowder strapped to their legs and arms. Instead of a slow sizzle there was just a quick bang and their bits were splattered. That was the idea, but it didn't always work.

Mary ordered 274 men, women and children to die at the stake.

Harrison's horrors

William Harrison wrote about everyday life in Tudor England. He also looked at crime and punishment:

Treason

The greatest crime in England at that time was treason – plotting against king and country. So the punishment was most horrible. Harrison said…

The greatest and most painful punishment used in England is for men who plot against the government or the monarch. The guilty man is drawn from the prison to the place of execution on a sled, where they are hanged till they be half dead. They are then taken down, and cut into quarters; after that, their bowels are cut from their bodies, and thrown into a fire, provided near at hand and within their own sight.

That's what happened to a man who tried to blow up Parliament with the king inside in 1605. The man, of course, was Guy Fawkes. Even today, 400 years later, the burning of his corpse is acted out every 5 November on Bonfire Night.

Murder

It wasn't enough to execute a murderer in Tudor times. The killer had to be killed so everyone could see them – and they'd be left there for a long time to remind you: 'This is what happens to murderers.'

Harrison said…

> *If a man be guilty of wilful murder he may be hanged alive in chains near the place where the murder was done. (Or, if the judge is kind, first strangled with a rope.) And there he stays till his bones rot to nothing.*

Suicide

You may think you can't be punished once you are dead. Wrong. In Tudor England people who killed themselves were criminals whose 'crime' was to have thrown away the life God had given them. They were punished by being buried outside the churchyard – Harrison said…

> *Those who kill themselves are buried in a field with a stake driven through their bodies.*

Very often, the suicide was buried at the crossroads with a stake through the heart. Why the crossroads? So if the ghost rose from its grave it wouldn't know which road to take to get home and haunt its family.

Poisoning

King Henry VIII brought in one especially cruel punishment just out of spite. The Bishop of Rochester's cook poisoned two of the Bishop's guests with a dinner he cooked. Henry ordered that the cook be boiled alive in his own pot. The law said killers had to be hanged. So horrid

Henry had the law changed. For five years in Henry's reign, poisoners were boiled alive. Hot stuff.

Did you know…?
Young Tudor men were not allowed to have long hair. Anyone convicted was sentenced to jail … *and* had to have a basin put over their head and their hair chopped off along the edges!

Jolly jail fever

The trouble with jails in Tudor times was that they were filthy places. You could go to jail for a short sentence – and come out in a box, dead from fever.

In Oxford, in 1577, almost everyone in court was wiped out with the sickness. The judges died, the juries died, the witnesses died. Three hundred people died. Who escaped with their lives? Was it…

a) the women spectators?
b) the police officers?
c) the prisoners?

Answer:
c) The prisoners lived in the filth and their bodies were used to it. When they came to court they passed on the disease to everyone else but they lived. Jail fever is called 'typhus' by doctors.

Escape from the terrible Tower

Here's a simple board game for those winter nights. So why not throw another chair on the fire and stretch out in front of its flickering warmth like a prisoner on a rack?

You need a dice and a playing partner. The first to reach the end can have a day off school! (But the day off must be a Sunday.) The loser must suffer the ghastly goat torture (from the Murderous Middle Ages).

13 Lady Jane Grey was executed at the Tower for taking Mary Tudor's throne. How long did Jane hang on to the throne?
a) 9 days
b) 9 weeks

14 A Tower raven dies. Bad luck. Go back to square 9.

15 Walter Raleigh laid his head on the block for the chop and got a message from the king. What did it say?
a) Serves you right
b) Only joking, keep your head on

12 Anne Boleyn's ghost tells you of a secret passage. Crawl forward to square 15.

11 Henry VIII's second wife, Anne Boleyn, was beheaded at the Tower. How?
a) with a slice of a sword
b) with a chop of an axe

10 Henry VIII clears his dungeons by executing all prisoners. Go back to start without your head.

START

1 Who built the Tower?
a) William the Conqueror
b) William the Torturer

2 A kind jailer's daughter gives you food. Throw dice again.

3 Who made Traitor's Gate collapse as it was being built?
a) Thomas a Becket's ghost
b) Viking raiders

You start in the Tower of London – one of the most haunted and horrible prisons in history. Take turns rolling the dice and move on the number of spaces shown. If you land on a question and get it right a) award yourself a tasty roast rat from the dungeon and b) throw again, but if you get it wrong a) award youself some water covered in dungeon slime and b) miss a turn. Throw the exact number to finish the game on the 'Freedom' square. Easy!

21 FREEDOM! You are free! Free to go to school. Come to think of it, you were probably better off in the Tower, weren't you?

20 You are on the last step to freedom – but slip on some blood. Tumble back to square 11.

19 The last execution at the Tower was when?
a) 1841
b) 1941

16 You find a diamond from the Crown jewels and bribe a guard. Go to square 19.

17 Colonel Blood stole the Crown Jewels by dressing up to fool the chief guard. He dressed as what?
a) a priest
b) a woman

18 Queen Victoria decides to pardon you as you've been in prison for 300 years. Throw again.

9 Two princes disappeared in 1483 – last seen in the Tower. 150 years later two little bodies were uncovered. Where?
a) in the Tower well
b) under the Tower stairs

8 You are stretched on the rack so thin you can slip through the bars and escape. Move on to square 11.

7 What appeared in the Tower in 1303 for the first time?
a) chopping blocks
b) the Crown jewels

4 A dungeon rat chews through your ropes and sets you free. Go to square 7.
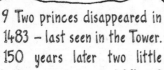

5 Welsh Prince Gruffydd died in the Tower. How?
a) he was beheaded with a saw
b) he fell out of a tower trying to escape

6 A fellow prisoner betrays your escape plan and you are locked in chains. Go back to start.

Answers:

1a) The White Tower was built in about 1078 by Bishop Gundulf for William the Conqueror.

3a) In 1240 a storm wrecked the building work of King Henry III. Thomas a Becket had been murdered on the orders of Henry's grandfather and Thomas's ghost was seen wandering the walls, making threats, just before the storm. Ooooh!

5b) The Tower was being used as a prison by about 1232. Welsh Prince Gruffydd was sent there in 1241 for being a rebel. He tried breaking out in 1244 – but ended up breaking his neck. Oooof!

7b) The Crown jewels were kept there in 1303 and they still are – but not the same jewels.

9b) Many people reckon King Richard III ordered the murder of his nephews aged 10 and 12. They were locked in a Tower cell and smothered in the night. Then buried under stones at the foot of some stairs and dug up later. Yeuch!

11a) Henry was being 'kind' to Anne because the sword was quicker and cleaner than the axe – bad axemen often took several hacks. It's said her lips were still moving after her head hit the floor. What was she saying? 'I'll be back to haunt you!' Some people reckon her ghost can still be seen there.

13a) The execution was really cruel. Instead of getting it over with quickly, poor Jane had to watch her husband taken off to execution first. She then had to watch his dead body brought back on a cart – with his head wrapped in a cloth. Jane was just 16 years old. Ahhhh!

15b) James I sent Raleigh for execution in 1603 – then spared him at the last moment. Fifteen years later James changed his mind and Raleigh went for the chop again. This time he was not spared. Splatt!

17a) In 1671 the jewels were nicked by Irishman Colonel Blood. Then Blood was nicked by the law men. When King Charles met Blood the Colonel had the cheek to tell the king that the Crown jewels weren't really worth that much. They were worth £100,000 but Blood said he wouldn't give £6,000 for them. The king forgave him.

19b) During the Second World War, people suspected of being enemy spies were imprisoned in the Tower. They were also executed by a firing squad if they were found guilty. Pow!

WILD WOMEN

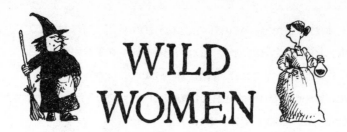

It's a fact that in history most crimes have been committed by men. It's also a fact that women have often been the victims of crime – and sometimes they've been punished for crimes they didn't even commit. Like the crime of being a witch. The story of witch hunts is a grim one...

A MESSAGE FROM OUR **HORRIBLE HISTORIES** AUTHOR...

LET'S GET THIS STRAIGHT. WITCHCRAFT IS NONSENSE - WITCHES DON'T FLY AROUND ON BROOMSTICKS. AND THEY DON'T TURN PEOPLE INTO FROGS...

POW!

OH YES WE DO!

RIBBET!

PEOPLE HAVE BELIEVED IN WITCHES SINCE THE EARLIEST TIMES.

THEY THOUGHT THE DEVIL COULD ENTER A HUMAN BODY AND PERFORM ALL SORTS OF EVIL MAGIC.

THE BEST WAY TO DESTROY THE EVIL WAS TO BURN THE BODY OF THE WITCH.

FROM 1450 TO 1598 OVER 30,000 PEOPLE BURNED AS WITCHES.

Spotting a witch

WITCHES DON'T ALL LOOK LIKE THEY DO IN KIDS' FAIRY TALE BOOKS - IF THEY DID IT WOULD BE EASY TO SPOT THEM.

IN GERMANY IN 1486 THE PEOPLE WERE GIVEN HELP IN WITCH-FINDING. A BOOK CALLED 'HAMMER OF THE WITCHES' SAID...

A witch is usually a woman or girl who...
~ has misty eyes
~ often kills and eats babies
~ often has red hair
~ can change herself into a bird or animal
~ fails to attend church
~ can fly on a broomstick or a goat
~ dislikes men
~ is friendly with animals – 'familiars' – who serve her

Testing a witch

MANY OF THE ACCUSED WERE OLD AND HELPLESS. BUT FIRST THEY HAD TO BE 'TESTED'. THE HAMMER OF THE WITCHES' SAID...

Witches hate water – and water hates witches. A witch must be tied – right hand to left foot, left hand to right foot – and thrown into a river. If she floats then it is because the water dislikes her taste and pushes her up. The witch is taken out and put on trial. If she sinks then she is innocent. She is taken out and released … but by then she could well have drowned.

Witch trials

WITCHES WERE USUALLY TORTURED UNTIL THEY OWNED UP.

IN ENGLAND IN 1645 JOAN WILLFORD'S CONFESSION SAID...

I admit that seven years ago the Devil appeared to me in the shape of a small dog and asked me to worship him.

EVENTUALLY, SOME PEOPLE HAD THE SENSE TO SEE THAT TORTURING OLD WOMEN WAS CRUEL AND NOT THE WAY TO DISCOVER THE TRUTH. FRANCIS HUTCHINSON WROTE 'AN ESSAY CONCERNING WITCHCRAFT' IN 1718.

Imagine a poor old woman, weak with old age, sitting like a fool in the middle of a room. There is a howling mob from ten towns around her house. Then her legs are tied in a cross so that the flow of blood is stopped and her sitting becomes painful. So she stays for 24 hours with no sleep, no food. No wonder that she confesses to anything. Any tales they invent about her, and much more as well.

Did you know…?
In the Middle Ages witches were often tried by the Bible. If they weighed more than the Bible they were set free – but the Bibles could be pretty heavy books in those days.

Witch-finders

WORST OF ALL WERE THE WITCH-FINDERS!

SO, WITCH-FINDERS LIED AND CHEATED AND MADE A FORTUNE.

WITCH-FINDERS WANTED

TRAVEL!
You could be sent anywhere in the country to find witches.

RICHES!
You will be paid for every witch found.

ADVENTURE!
Catch them.
Try them.
See them hang.

SERVE YOUR COUNTRY

APPLY TO: MATTHEW HOPKINS
WITCH-FINDER GENERAL OF ENGLAND 1645-1646

Witch-finders Weekly

Trick pricker

The best way to prove you've got a witch is to find the Devil's Mark on your suspect's skin. For this you use a 'pricker', don't you?

But what if you prick and prick and don't find the spot? Then use our super new trick pricker!

Here's how it works:

- The point is placed on the victim.
- The handle is pushed down.
- The point slips back into the handle.
- It appears that the point has gone into the skin and found a Devil's Mark.

Now you can charge the witch and prove her guilty.

Matthew Hopkins himself says:

If you can't prick her then trick her! It works for me.

Buy your trick pricker at your nearest witch-finder shop. Still only three groats. Buy one and try one – you won't be disappointed.

MATTHEW HOPKINS HAD HUNDREDS EXECUTED USING THAT TRICK... THEN HE WAS EXECUTED HIMSELF FOR HIS LYING AND CRUELTY.

CAN'T SAY I'M SORRY.

IN FACT YOU COULD SAY...

SERVED HIM RIGHT!

SOME PEOPLE BELIEVE THAT HORRIBLE HOPKINS DIED QUIETLY IN HIS BED. IT WOULD BE A PITY IF THAT WERE TRUE!

Did you know…?

In America in 1692 a witch hunt in Salem led to the deaths of 19 suspects. The accusers said 'sorry' four years later! They wrote:

> *We confess our sorrow for our mistakes. We humbly beg forgiveness of God and all of you whom we have offended. We declare we would not do such things again.*

It was a bit too late then. The victims were too dead to forgive the accusers.

Sin sense

In the 1500s a prayer was written which shows that not everyone was as stupidly superstitious as the rest. The prayer says what we know today – these 'witches' weren't killed because they practised magic or dealt with the Devil. Their *real* sin was something else…

For all those who died – stripped naked, shaved, shorn.

For those who screamed in vain to God, only to have their tongues ripped out by the root.

For those who were pricked, racked, broken on the wheel for the sins of the witch-hunters.

For those whose beauty stirred their torturers to fury.

For those whose ugliness did the same.

For those who were neither ugly nor beautiful, but only women who would not confess.

For those quick fingers broken in the vice.

For those soft arms pulled from their sockets.

For all those witch-women, my sisters, who breathed freer as the flames took them, knowing as they shed their female bodies, that death would shed them of the sin for which they died – the sin of being born a woman.

The branks

Women didn't only suffer when accused of witchcraft. Ordinary women in Britain have also suffered horrible punishments just for nagging a husband or talking too much. In the 1500s, such a woman could be fitted with the brutal 'branks' – also known as the 'Scold's Bridle'.

- The branks was a steel cage worn on the head like a helmet.
- Inside the cage was a steel plate that either had sharp spikes on it or which was cruelly sharpened.

- This plate was placed in the offending woman's mouth so that if she even moved her tongue she would do major damage to her mouth and tongue and suffer terrible pain.
- The woman had to wear this cage in town.
- Sometimes a chain was fixed to the front of the branks so that she could be led around like a dog on a leash.

Gutsy Grace – crime pays

Women haven't always been victims. Take Grace O'Malley from Ireland. She was famous as a pirate – and a friend of Queen Elizabeth I. There are many legends about her adventures. She has become a sort of female Robin Hood in Ireland – a criminal, but a good one. Here's her story…

Howth Castle, near Dublin, Ireland, 1590
The wind whipped off the Irish Sea and tugged at the cloak of the woman on the horse. 'Not far now,' she called over the wail of the wind. 'Howth Castle in half a mile and shelter for the night!'

The woman looked strong as a bear under that great grey cloak and her face was hard as the rocks on the road. The man nodded, shivered inside his leather jerkin and spurred his tired horse up the hill.

Howth Castle towered above them and the massive walls sheltered them from the wind. As the woman reached the mighty oak gates a servant in a beetle-black suit scuttled across the castle yard. The woman smiled at him. 'Good evening,' she said.

The servant wrinkled his pale face in a sour snarl. 'Stand back! Stand back, I say! I need to close the gates. It's sunset. Have to close the gates.'

The woman raised a hand as the servant grasped the gate. 'I am Grace O'Malley. I am captain of one of Queen Elizabeth's ships. I come to visit the Lord of Howth.'

The servant pulled back his bloodless lips in a broken-toothed sneer. 'Well, you're too late! His lordship has started dinner. It's more than my job's worth to disturb him now.'

With a flick of his frail wrists the servant swung the door shut and Grace's startled horse reared up. By the time her bodyguard in the leather jerkin had helped her calm it, the bars had been slammed into place.

The woman's weather-worn face was pale with fury. She turned and walked her horse down the hill towards Dublin bay. 'A fine welcome, Mallen,' she said. 'We must repay the Lord of Howth's kindness some day.'

'Yes, ma'am,' Mallen murmured but his words were whisked away by the biting wind. They bent their heads into the stinging rain and didn't see the horsemen riding towards them till they almost crashed into them. The boy they met pulled his pony to a halt and slid from the saddle. He looked up at Grace O'Malley's fierce face and grinned. 'Sorry! I'm in a hurry to get home!'

'What home would that be?' the woman asked.

'Howth Castle,' the boy said. 'I'm Robyn, son of the Lord of Howth.'

Grace O'Malley turned her head slowly and looked at Mallen. The man in the leather jacket understood. He jumped down, grasped the boy and helped him back into his saddle. Then he took the reins and held them as he climbed back on to his own horse. He began to lead the boy down the hill.

The boy's servant, on a grey donkey, was confused. 'He's going the wrong way!' he cried.

Grace O'Malley leaned forward. From under her cloak a dagger appeared and it was at the throat of the startled servant before he could blink.

'Now, my little donkey,' she said, 'you can choose. Take a message to the Lord of Howth or have your throat cut.'

'Take a … take a … take a message,' the man babbled.

'Tell his lordship Grace O'Malley called for shelter and supper tonight. I was turned away from his door. There is an old Irish custom that says you always leave your door open and always have a spare place at your table for a weary traveller. His son will be on my ship. He can agree to lay that place at his table or I will drop his son into the Irish Sea. Understand?'

'Yes – yes.' The man dug his heels into the donkey and the animal trotted up the rocky road and disappeared into the gloom and mist.

When the mists had cleared and the morning sun sparkled on Dublin Bay a small boat rowed out to Grace O'Malley's ship.

The Lord of Howth's servant was helped aboard and led before the captain. The man bowed his back and didn't dare look her in the eye. 'Captain O'Malley, I bring a message from the Lord of Howth.'

The woman nodded.

'His lordship says you are welcome to dine with him – at any time. There will always be a spare place set at the table in Howth castle.'

That all happened four hundred years ago, they say. But if you go to Howth Castle today you will find there is an extra place at the table.

Did you know…?
The last stagecoach robber in America was a woman – Pearl Hart. She escaped from prison in 1899 but was captured again. When she was pardoned in 1902 she disappeared without a trace...

Woman's weapon

Some people say poison is a woman's weapon – men will usually shoot or stab or beat a victim to death but a woman prefers to poison her victim. That's certainly been true of some killers. Take the case of Mrs Doss…

THE WOMAN WHO PRUNED HER HUSBAND

Samuel Doss died in Tulsa, Oklahoma, in 1954, after eating a plate of prunes. The police doctor examined the body and found enough poison in his stomach to kill ten men.

Mrs Doss was shocked. 'How on earth did that happen?' she wanted to know.

The police replied, 'We thought you may had slipped the poison in the prunes.'

'My conscience is clear,' she said.

They then did a little digging into her past and found she'd had three husbands before Doss who had died after stomach pains … and so had her mother, and a sister and two of her children had died suspiciously.

She was one of those poisoners who just kept on poisoning until she was caught. Many famous poisoners seem to fall into that trap – poisoning becomes a habit they can't break.

EVIL
18TH CENTURY

Killing someone for a crime is an odd thing to do when you think about it…

YOU WILL BE EXECUTED FOR BREAKING THAT WINDOW!

THAT WON'T MEND THE WINDOW!

Executing a criminal is too late to stop the crime.

EXECUTING YOU WILL TEACH YOU THAT YOU CAN'T BREAK WINDOWS!

NO IT WON'T… I'LL BE TOO DEAD TO REMEMBER THAT LESSON.

Some people still believe in 'capital punishment' – death for some crimes. The reasons they give for murdering another human are…

IF YOU'RE DEAD YOU WON'T BE ABLE TO REPEAT YOUR CRIME!

YOUR DEATH WILL PUT OTHER CRIMINALS OFF CRIME!

AND WE JUST WANT REVENGE!

Hanging off

There have been some horribly historical executions in the past… In the 18th century the law tried to be terribly tough and hanged people for just about anything. In fact, by the 18th century, 222 crimes could be punished by hanging. Steal something worth more than five shillings (25p) from a shop? You're hanged. Steal anything from a shipwreck? You're hanged. You could even be hanged if you were caught cutting down a tree or robbing a rabbit warren. But the punishment was *so* harsh

it didn't always work. Often, the jury would look at the criminal and decide…

The jury didn't want to see a criminal hanged for a small offence so they let them off. That meant criminals were getting away with it, and the law had to change. From 1823 to 1837, a hundred of the hanging crimes were changed so that the criminals went to prison instead.

Hang around for a party

In London, prisoners were taken to chapel on the Sunday morning before they were hanged. They sat round an empty coffin while a priest told them how wicked they were. Next day they were taken in open carts to Tyburn (now Marble Arch) where large crowds gathered. It was like a street party – a good day out known as 'Tyburn Fair'. There was food and drink on sale and grandstand seats for a good view.

A poet called John Taylor wrote this dreadful ditty about Tyburn gallows. He compared Tyburn gallows to a fruit tree…

John from
5H

The Tyburn Tree, it does appear,
Has dangling fruit twelve times a year.
It has no leaf, no roots, no bud,
The rain that makes it grow is blood.
I find this tree has never been
Like other fruit trees all fenced in.
But by the roadside stands for years
Yet no one steals the fruit, I hear.
I've seen this dead fruit, noted it,
Not put in jam but in a pit.
Like all bad fruit both far and wide
It's eaten by the worms inside.

> *Did you know...?*
>
> The bodies of executed criminals, especially highwaymen, were often hung in chains to rot at the scene of their crimes. A 'gibbet' used for this sort of hanging is still on show at Caxton near Huntingdon.

Grave crimes

The bodies of some hanged criminals went to the doctors – not to be cured, but to be cut up for experiments. Surgeons were allowed to practise on the dead bodies of criminals but no one else. (The 1752 law said any executed criminal could be used.) Criminals could be brave about being hanged – but were terrified at the thought of being cut up after they were dead.

But there weren't enough hanged bodies to satisfy some doctors. They started to pay good money for a fresh corpse – and they didn't ask questions about where you got that body from. So a new crime grew in the 1700s – bodysnatching. Men robbed graves and sold the corpses to the surgeons.

The two most famous 'bodysnatchers' were Burke and Hare ... but they never 'snatched' a single body! They ran a lodging house in Edinburgh for the poor. When they found a poor person alone they would offer them a bed for the night ... then smother them to death and sell the body. Burke and Hare weren't really bodysnatchers, they were murderers. They were caught, and in 1829 Burke was hanged. Hare went free because he gave evidence against his former partner.

Perhaps the most ruthless bodysnatcher was Andrew Merrilees. In 1818 his sister died. He sold her to the doctors! Would you do that to your sister? Better not answer that, on second thoughts.

Bodysnatching ended when a new law was passed in 1832 that allowed doctors to experiment legally on many other bodies. They no longer needed to risk buying from bodysnatchers so the terrible trade died out.

Heads you lose, Cath

In the savage 1700s ordinary killers were hanged. BUT a woman who killed her husband was NOT just a killer (the law said), she was guilty of 'treason' – a crime against the whole of the country. So she should be burned alive. This wasn't the Middle Ages and this wasn't a case of witchcraft. This was just over 250 years ago. Surely they wouldn't burn a woman alive in those days?

Want to bet? Look at the case of Catherine Hayes. If Catherine had had a nosey neighbour then a letter may have looked like this...

London

9 May 1726

Dear Mum,

Hope you are well. You'll never believe what happened next door to us. Well, you remember that nice John Hayes who lived there? He disappeared a month ago and we all thought it was a bit odd. Then something happened so disgusting I don't think I should tell you about it, but I will.

A head turned up in a pond in Marylebone, just down the road. Now the law officers didn't know who the dead head belonged to, so you'll never believe what they did? They stuck it on a pole and put it on show in St Margaret's churchyard in Westminster. Horrible or what? It made me shiver just to think about it. But thousands of people were going to have a look at it and I went along with John Hayes's wife – Catherine. Remember her? You said you didn't like her the moment you met her.

Off we went to look at the head and as soon as I saw it I cried, 'Eeeeh! Catherine! That's your John!'

The hair on the dead head had all been nicely washed and the head was in a glass case but I knew it was him.

Everybody turns and looks at us and Catherine's really annoyed.

'No it's not, you ignorant sow,' she says to me.

'It is! I tell you! It is. That's John Hayes, as I live and breathe.'

Suddenly Catherine screams. 'It is! It's my husband. Oh, my poor John!' She snatches the glass case down from the pole and starts cuddling it and sobbing and wailing. What a performance!

Well, the law officers talk to her while I go home. The next thing I know they've arrested someone for the murder. I said to my George, 'I hear they've arrested someone.'

And he says, smug as a cat with a nest of rats, 'I know. And I know who they've arrested.'

'Who?' I gasped.

Well, I nearly swallowed me tongue when he told me. 'Catherine Hayes!'

'Catherine's his wife,' I laughed. 'She wouldn't murder her husband...' I started to say. Then I looked at my fat, idle slob of a husband and thought, 'I don't know though!'

Anyway, she went to trial. It seems she and a partner killed John to rob him and cut off the head to stop his corpse being recognized. Didn't work, did it?

They found her guilty and of course the punishment for killing your husband isn't hanging, is it? No. It's to be burned at the stake. It's enough to put any woman off chopping up her old man.

It's so horrible. I wouldn't want to see her sizzle and fry. But she was my next-door neighbour so I suppose I'll have to go and watch.

Hope you and Dad are keeping well. Look forward to you coming to see us next month when I'll tell you how the execution went.

Your loving daughter,

Isobel

Catherine Hayes was burned alive on 9 May 1726. The executioner was supposed to strangle her as she stood chained to the stake to put her out of her misery. But the flames leapt up and burned his hands before he could finish her off. She tried to kick away the burning wood but more was thrown on. She died slowly and painfully.

Did you know...?
In 1785, 97 people were executed in England. How many of those were for murder and how many for burglary?
a) 96 for murder, 1 for burglary
b) 50 for murder, 47 for burglary
c) 1 for murder, 96 for burglary

Answer:

c) Many of those executed were children under fifteen. In 1801 a boy of thirteen was hanged for breaking into a house and stealing a spoon.

Poisonous pirates and hideous highwaymen

The 1700s were a great time for pirates and highwaymen. These vicious criminals (men and women) would torture, wound or kill to get their hands on other people's money. Yet today pirates and highwaymen have become jolly figures in children's books – Robin Hoods of the seas and the roads. They weren't. They were usually heartless and selfish and they were punished savagely when they were caught.

Newspapers became popular in the 1700s. So here are a few hideous headlines for you to read – except some words are missing. Can you fit them in?

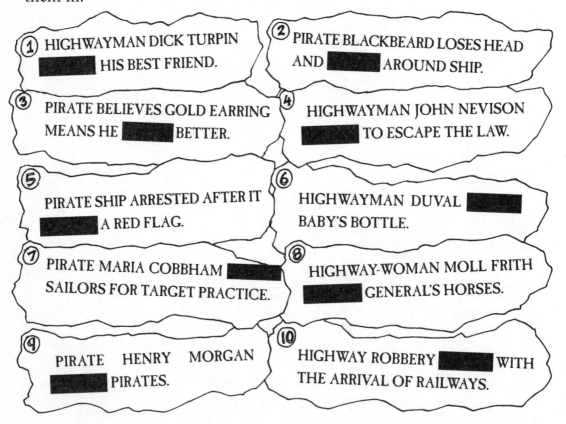

1. HIGHWAYMAN DICK TURPIN ▮▮▮ HIS BEST FRIEND.

2. PIRATE BLACKBEARD LOSES HEAD AND ▮▮▮ AROUND SHIP.

3. PIRATE BELIEVES GOLD EARRING MEANS HE ▮▮▮ BETTER.

4. HIGHWAYMAN JOHN NEVISON ▮▮▮ TO ESCAPE THE LAW.

5. PIRATE SHIP ARRESTED AFTER IT ▮▮▮ A RED FLAG.

6. HIGHWAYMAN DUVAL ▮▮▮ BABY'S BOTTLE.

7. PIRATE MARIA COBBHAM ▮▮▮ SAILORS FOR TARGET PRACTICE.

8. HIGHWAY-WOMAN MOLL FRITH ▮▮▮ GENERAL'S HORSES.

9. PIRATE HENRY MORGAN ▮▮▮ PIRATES.

10. HIGHWAY ROBBERY ▮▮▮ WITH THE ARRIVAL OF RAILWAYS.

MISSING WORDS: DROPS OFF, USES, STEALS, RIDES, SWIMS, SEES, KILLS, SHOOTS, CATCHES, FLIES

Answers:

1 Shoots. Turpin went to rescue his friend, Matthew King, who had been arrested. As he took aim at the law officer through the window, Matthew King stood up – and was hit by the bullet instead. Ooops! (Dick Turpin is remembered as a gentleman-thief. He wasn't. He once roasted a tavern keeper over a fire to make her tell where her savings were hidden.)

2 Swims. Blackbeard was caught by the Royal Navy and shot. To finish him off the navy officer cut off his head and threw Blackbeard's corpse over the side of the ship. It's said the headless body swam once around the ship before it sank. Believe that if you like!

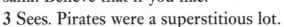

3 Sees. Pirates were a superstitious lot. A gold ear-ring helped them to see in the dark (they thought).

4 Rides. Some people believe the story that Dick Turpin rode his horse Black Bess from London to York in a day to escape the law. He didn't. That was a story written in a novel called *Rookwood* after Turpin died. But it is said that highwayman Nevison *did* make this incredible journey and it saved him – for a while.

5 Flies. Not many pirate ships flew the skull-and-crossbones flag you see in children's books. A black flag usually meant 'Stop right there or we'll come and get you.' If a ship ignored it then the pirate hoisted a red flag that meant, 'Right, you've been warned – we're coming to get you!'

6 Steals. Duval was supposed to be a 'gentleman' – and robbed ladies in stagecoaches very politely. But he wasn't so polite to babies and once stole a baby's feeding bottle because it was silver.

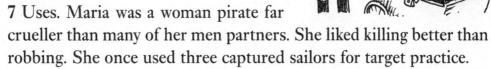

7 Uses. Maria was a woman pirate far crueller than many of her men partners. She liked killing better than robbing. She once used three captured sailors for target practice.

8 Kills. Moll Frith escaped from robbing General Fairfax by shooting him and killing his two horses. She was later arrested but paid £2,000 to get free. Marvellous Moll had a play written about her called *The Roaring Girl* and managed to die peacefully of old age.

9 Catches. Morgan was a pirate in the West Indies. The king of England met him and sent Morgan back to the West Indies to be governor of Jamaica with the job of catching and hanging pirates. He made a good job of it. As the old proverb says, 'Set a thief to catch a thief'.

10 Drops off. Stage coaches were slow and easy to stop. Once they were replaced by the railways in the mid-1800s highwaymen were soon out of a job. Though, in 1963, the Great Train Robbery in southern England was a bit like the old highway robbery – the train was stopped with a fake signal, the driver clubbed to the ground and the guards tied up.

Did you know…?
The Bishop of Raphoe was a highwayman in his spare time. He made one big mistake when he held up a coach where the passenger was armed with a pistol. The passenger shot the bishop dead. Hope he went to heaven.

TEST
YOUR TEACHER

Teachers are very clever people. They know a lot about everything. But they know most of all about 'history'. That's because most teachers are so old they were there when those things happened. So your teacher will be happy to answer these simple questions on executions…

1 In America the electric chair is still used to shock people to death. Who invented it?

a) A teacher.

b) A dentist.

c) An electrician.

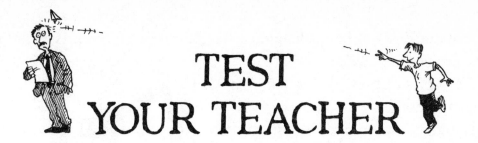

2 The French liked the guillotine for painless beheadings. But one doctor said the chopped head lived on for 30 seconds. How did this daft doctor try to prove it?

a) He called out the name of the victim and looked to see if the head opened its eyes.

b) He fixed wires to the head and checked that brainwaves were still going.

c) He punched the head on the nose and watched it screw up with the pain.

3 Spanish soldiers captured Inca king Atahualpa and said they'd burn him alive if he didn't become a Christian. As he was led out to be executed he said he wanted to become a Christian. What did the Spanish do?

a) Set him free.

b) Burned him anyway.

c) Granted his wish and *didn't* burn him … but strangled him instead.

4 From the 1930s, Britain's hangman was Albert Pierrepont. Why did he pack his job up in 1956?

a) He was so upset by his job that he hanged himself.

b) Hanging was stopped in Britain and poor old Albert was out of a job.

c) He had a row about his wages and refused to hang any more.

5 In England, in 1884, John Lee became known as 'The Man They Could Not Hang'. Why?

a) They couldn't catch him to hang him – he kept escaping.

b) Every time they tried to hang him the scaffold jammed.

c) Because John Lee's dad, Albert Lee, was the hangman and he said, 'This is the man I cannot hang.'

6 In the Middle Ages, animals could be brought to trial and executed if they were found guilty. How did they appear in court?

a) Dressed in human clothes.

b) With a rope around the neck ready to be hanged.

c) With a trough of food to keep them quiet.

7 In ancient Rome an executioner could not go on hacking till someone's head came off. They were only allowed how many chops?

a) One.
b) Two.
c) Three.

8 The Scottish rebel, William Wallace, has become known as 'Braveheart'. He was executed in London in 1305 and became a famous first. How?

a) He was the first person to have his head stuck on a pole over London Bridge.

b) He was the first Scotsman to be executed under the law which said 'You must not wear a kilt on a Bank Holiday Monday'.

c) He was the first person to have his lungs chopped up for haggis.

9 Another rebel Scotsman, Lord Lovat, was the last person to be beheaded in public in Britain in 1747. Twenty others died with him. How?
a) They were all beheaded too – heads all over the place.
b) They came to watch from a wooden stand and it collapsed.
c) They were killed by robbers who stabbed them in the packed crowds.

10 Doctors liked executions because they could experiment on the criminal corpses. But in 1803 Professor Aldini tried an odd experiment on the criminal corpse of George Foster. What did he do?
a) He did the world's first heart transplant.
b) He cooked his heart and ate it for dinner.
c) He tried to bring him back to life.

Answers:

1b) Dentist Alfred Southwick was interested in electricity. He thought it could be useful to him as a dentist – maybe (he thought) a quick shock would knock someone out while I pull their tooth out. Then a man in Buffalo town stumbled into an electric generator and was killed. Southwick got an idea – death from electricity was a quick, painless way to die. He and a doctor, George Fell, tested this on animals in 1882. By 1889 New York criminals were being executed – but they found it wasn't quick or painless.

(In 1890 the Emperor of Abyssinia, Menelek II, decided to bring his country up to date. He ordered three electric chairs from the United States for executions. Then he discovered that you needed *electricity* to make them work but there was *no* electricity in Abyssinia at that time. He had two chairs scrapped. The third he kept … as his throne!)
2a) The daft doctor was believed for many years but it's just not true.

3c) Spanish leader Pizarro said, 'Atahualpa was punished for his great wrongs and cruelties. The Inca people said that he was the cruellest butcher that had ever been known, and that he would burn a village to the ground for a small crime committed by one of its villagers, and kill ten thousand people.'

4c) Pierrepont executed 450 people between 1931 and 1956. (He learned how to do it by helping his dad Henry and his uncle Tom.) His victims included Ruth Ellis, the last woman to be hanged in Britain in 1955. Then, in 1956, Albert went to a prison to hang a man – only to find the man had been let off. Albert wanted his £15 hanging fee, but the Prison Service only gave him £1 for his bus fares. Albert was furious. They later sent him another £4 but the noose-knotter had had enough. He never hanged again.

5b) John Lee killed his old employer and was sentenced to death. 'God will never allow me to be executed,' he said. He had seen it in a dream. He was placed on the scaffold, a rope round his neck. But when the lever was pulled the trapdoor didn't open. He was taken away, and the scaffold was tested. It worked perfectly. Twice more they tried to hang him and the machinery stuck each time. He was given life in prison instead.

6a) Animals were dressed in human clothes for their trial. Since they couldn't speak for themselves, they were given a lawyer to speak for them.

7c) Saint Cecilia was sentenced to death for being a Christian. She laughed at her judge so he said she should be suffocated to death in her own steam bath – but she survived. So then a soldier chopped at her head three times – but she survived that too, though she was horribly wounded. He had to stop the chop because he was only allowed three strikes. She lived on for three days before she died. At least she went to heaven with her head on – just.

8a) Willie Wallace's head decorated London Bridge and that became a popular thing – especially with the London crows who liked to peck out the eyes for dinner or pull out the hair to make a nest.

9b) Lord Lovat enjoyed his execution. Well, he was 80 years old and hadn't long to go anyway. So when the crowd shouted insults at him he shouted them back. The stand built to hold the crowds collapsed and 20 of his English enemy died in the crush. Old Lovat must have *really* enjoyed that! Almost worth getting executed for!

10c) Professor Aldini had seen how electricity could make dead animals twitch as if they were alive. He decided to try putting electricity through George's corpse to bring him back to life. Of course, hospitals still use electric shocks to bring patients back to life and it often works. But, sadly for George, it didn't this time.

Did you know...?
A Danish writer wrote a book that said nasty things about Sweden – and Sweden was ruling Denmark at that time. So the Swedes gave the writer a choice:

What would *you* do?
The writer boiled the book in a pot of soup and ate it.

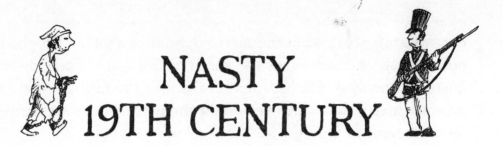

NASTY 19TH CENTURY

The 19th century was a prime crime time. In Britain, crime rates grew quickly as people crowded into towns and stole ... or starved. There were some pretty famous murderers around in the 1800s – and maybe the most famous of all was 'Jack the Ripper' who was never caught and punished. (But don't worry – if he's still alive he'll be about 150 years old by now and too wrinkly to rip anyone else.)

Still, there were now better police forces round the world with new crime-fighting weapons like fingerprint testing, photographs and bump-reading. (Yes, Dr Franz Joseph Gall of Vienna reckoned you could tell a criminal by feeling the bumps on their heads. Fingerprinting caught on – bump-reading didn't. You win some, you lose some.)

Most countries now got rid of 'public' executions – criminals were still hanged or chopped to death but in the peace and quiet of a prison, not outside as a public party.

Terrible treadmills

In 1818 British prisons started using 'treadmills'. These were like big hamster-wheels for prisoners to walk inside. Of course they never got anywhere. But it was exhausting. (Schools copied this cruel idea and still use it – they call it 'cross-country running'.)

Collars and cages

Prison can be hard anywhere at any time. But Chinese police stations were NOT the sort of place you'd care to be held in during the 1800s. A priest from Europe visited one and reported what he saw...

I came upon police stations, where criminals of different types were suffering different punishments. Some were simply imprisoned in large cages, to be jeered at by the passer-by. Others wore thick collars made of two wide boards brought together at their edges, with a hole large enough for the neck. The collar is so wide that the prisoner cannot reach his head with his hands, and needs the help of his friends to eat his food.

Others had their heads sticking out of the tops of cages which were so high that they could not sit down, and so low that they could not stand up. They were forced to spend days and nights in this awkward and even torturing position. A short time before, several criminals who had been guilty of a serious offence were sentenced to death, and placed in these cages. There they died from starvation, no one being allowed to pass them food.

Vile Voyevoask

In the 1800s the Russians sent their villains to Voyevoask, a prison camp in the frozen north, to work till they died. The Russian playwright Chekhov described some of the suffering…

When I arrived, the first thing I heard was complaints about bugs. You cannot live with them. At one time they were killed with lime, or they were frozen to death during intensely cold weather, but now nothing helps. Even the prison guards' quarters smell of toilets and filth and even they complain about the bugs.

Terrible transportation

When Britain's jails became full in the 1700s and 1800s the law started sending people to British 'colonies' and America and Australia became filled with British criminals. This was called 'transportation' and could be far worse than jail...

Five filthy facts about transportation

1 In the early 1800s there were over 200 crimes that could be punished with the death sentence. But many judges were not happy about hanging a man for small crimes. They were delighted that they could 'transport' a man, woman or child instead. In 1805 George Ainsley of Durham was sentenced to death for breaking in to a house and was sentenced to hang for it. Ainsley's sentence was changed. He was given 14 years in Australia instead of a noose.

2 The worst Australian convict-master was Major Joseph Foveaux who was in charge from 1800 to 1804. He flogged prisoners till their bones showed through the torn flesh then threw salt water over the wounds and sent the men straight back to work. He had leg irons made small so they cut into the ankles and he had a half-flooded punishment cell. If the prisoner dared to fall asleep he'd drown.

3 Judges had a choice between seven-year or 14-year sentences – nothing more, nothing less and nothing between. So Gordon Alexander was given seven years for stealing a pair of candlesticks in 1805 while Christopher Scorton got 14 years for stealing a horse. Barbara Oliver got 14 years for forging bank notes in 1816 while highwayman Christopher Humble Junior got just seven years a short while before her.

I'D HAVE BEEN BETTER OFF STEALING MONEY INSTEAD OF MAKING IT!

4 When criminals returned from Australia they weren't usually better people – but they were often better criminals! They learned lots of new tricks from the other convicts! Any who escaped a seven-year sentence and returned home would be sent back for 14 years. Anyone escaping a second time was hanged.

5 The oldest convict to be transported from Britain was 82-year-old Dorothy Handland. She survived the trip but hanged herself from a gum tree when she arrived. John Hudson stole some clothes and a gun and became the youngest person to be transported. He was nine years old. Transportation ended in 1868.

The transported criminals lived a savage life. And not only the convicts suffered. The first convicts arrived in Tasmania in 1802, where 20,000 native Tasmanians lived. Just 74 years later the last native Tasmanian died. A whole Tasmanian nation had been wiped out by brutal British convicts.

The story of the pitiful piper

There is a story told about old Durham jail in the north of England. You can still hear the ghost of a man who died there 200 years ago. The story goes like this…

Go down the steps at the end of Elvet Bridge. Go to the water's edge. That's the spot where the old jail opened on to the river.

Go at a quiet time and you may just hear the heartbreaking moan of bagpipes. If you do hear them then you'll know you are hearing a ghost.

It's the ghost of an old gypsy who was arrested in 1803. He'd had a long and wicked career as a horse-thief and at last the Durham magistrates had had enough of him. They wouldn't lock him up, this time. Instead, they sentenced him to transportation.

But he was an old man whose health was failing and he would never survive the three-month journey. The sentence was as good as a sentence to death. A slow, miserable death on board a stinking, rat-infested ship.

As it turned out, the old horse-thief never set foot on that ship. He was too weak to travel so he was kept in old Durham jail till he recovered. A year in the jail turned into two, then three. After seven years the Prince of Wales heard about the old man's suffering. Old King George, the Prince's father, was too mad to give a royal pardon so the Prince of Wales himself sent the pardon north from London.

It was a three day ride over rutted and muddy roads for the messenger. At last he reached Durham Jail. 'Take me to the governor of the jail!' he demanded. 'I come from the Prince!'

'The governor is busy,' he was told. 'He's arranging the funeral of an old gypsy horse-thief. He died just an hour ago!'

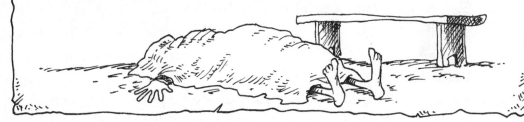

The brutal British army

British soldiers were often punished by being whipped. Sometimes up to 1,500 lashes and the victim could be killed. This flogging was stopped in Europe in the 18th century. In the British army it went on until 1881.

Until 1859 a deserter (someone who ran away from the army) would be tattooed on the left armpit with the letter 'D'. A soldier who made trouble would be tattooed with BC (Bad Character). The army used gunpowder and ink for the tattoos.

The Indians hated the harsh rule of the British and their army and in 1857 they had a mutiny. The British decided to execute the rebels cruelly as an example. The captured rebels were tied over the mouth of a loaded cannon and blown from it. And it wasn't just the men who enjoyed the massacre. Two vile Victorian women, dressed in white and seated on white horses, rode up just as one execution took place. As the Indian's head flew ten metres in the air they were splattered with his blood. They rode off proudly stained from head to toe in red.

Fearful Thugs

Those British soldiers had to be tough – they had to act as policemen around the British Empire. And they came across some sickening sights…

You may think human sacrifices were something that disappeared in ancient times but you'd be wrong. From the 1500s the Thuggees of India killed people as a sacrifice to their god Kali. Their favourite victims were travellers whom they killed and robbed. The Thuggees pretended to be friendly travellers and made their victims feel safe – then they strangled them as they slept.

The British took control of India in the 1830s and began to stop the Thuggee gang murders. Brit Colonel Sleeman wrote a book about the Kali killers in which he described capturing a Thuggee who confessed…

> We came to a river where we found four soldiers cooking. We murdered them. This took some time and was difficult… One of the soldiers must have guessed what we were up to and made such great efforts to save his life that he got away a few paces and raised his spear in defence. He was instantly overpowered and murdered.
>
> As we were resting close to where these soldiers had just met their fate, four strolling players joined us. We spoke kindly to them, promising to hear them sing and dance … we murdered them that night…

Pitiful plays

Those vile Victorians just loved going to the theatre to see plays based on cracking crime stories. The most popular play of the 19th century was probably *The Murder In The Red Barn*. This true story happened in Suffolk, England, in 1827, when rich William Corder promised to marry poor Maria Marten – but really planned to shoot her in the lonely Red Barn. Here is the famous scene where Corder meets her – prepare to boo and hiss!

Corder buried the girl and escaped. But one year later Maria appeared to her mother in a dream. The dead girl told of her murder. Corder was arrested and hanged.

Did you know…?

America's most famous killer of the 1800s was Lizzie Borden. When Lizzie was 32 years old she was accused of hacking her father and stepmother to death with an axe. All the proof pointed to her – yet she was found 'not guilty' and set free. Her story has been turned into a song, a ballet, a film and a musical.

Revolting riddle

Tommy Otter killed his girlfriend in Nottinghamshire in 1808. After he was executed (by hanging) his body was hung in chains at the place where he killed her. A Nottingham poet came up with this putrid riddle about what happened next. It's not easy though, so don't worry if you don't guess the answer in a hundred years!

> *Ten tongues in one head*
> *Nine living and one dead.*
> *One flew out to fetch some bread*
> *To feed the living in the head.*

Answer:

A blue-tit built its nest in Tom Otter's skull and raised eight chicks.

IT'S WARM OUT THERE.

BUT IT'S OTTER IN HERE!

Deadly doctors

A doctor's job is to cure people. But if you're a murderer who just happens to be a doctor, you're in luck. You've got lots of ways of killing people at your fingertips – and that's why there are so many deadly docs in history…

OOOPS! THE KNIFE MUST HAVE SLIPPED.

These days it's harder to get away with murder if you're a doctor – though in Britain in 2000 Doctor Harold Shipman managed to 'help' at least 200 patients to die before he was caught. In the past it was easier to get away with it – take the case of Dr Palmer in the 1800s. He came up with a wacky way to hide his crime and almost succeeded…

A doctor called Palmer murdered a friend called Cook in 1855 – his 14th victim. The police doctor examined the body – but the examination was a joke.

Palmer had been a friend of the dead man, and he was also a doctor, so he said, 'Mind if I watch while you look at the corpse?' The police doctor agreed.

Cook's stomach was full of strychnine poison and Palmer knew that – after all, he'd fed the poison to his friend. But, as the police doctor lifted the stomach from the body, Palmer gave him a push. The contents spilled on the floor! They couldn't be tested.

Poisonous Palmer may have escaped again but the police reported the death to the man who looks at suspicious deaths – the coroner. Palmer tried to bribe the coroner to say it was a natural death. Big mistake. The police at last became suspicious.

After other bodies had been examined, deadly Doctor Palmer was found guilty and executed.

Imagine having the nerve to splatter the poisoned stomach juices over the floor!

Daft detectives

In the 1800s, detectives started to use science to help solve cases. But in 1876 Cesare Lombardo of Italy came up with the daft idea that you can spot a criminal just by looking at him (or her). Lump-head Lombardo studied 7,000 criminals and came up with this…

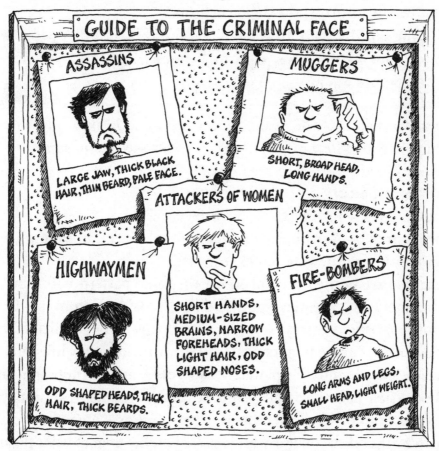

GUIDE TO THE CRIMINAL FACE

ASSASSINS
LARGE JAW, THICK BLACK HAIR, THIN BEARD, PALE FACE.

MUGGERS
SHORT, BROAD HEAD, LONG HANDS.

ATTACKERS OF WOMEN
SHORT HANDS, MEDIUM-SIZED BRAINS, NARROW FOREHEADS, THICK LIGHT HAIR, ODD SHAPED NOSES.

HIGHWAYMEN
ODD SHAPED HEADS, THICK HAIR, THICK BEARDS.

FIRE-BOMBERS
LONG ARMS AND LEGS, SMALL HEAD, LIGHT WEIGHT.

Lombardo may have studied 7,000 criminals – but he didn't study 7 million ordinary people. If he had he'd have found that there are thousands of people with short heads and long hands who are *not* muggers.

Fingerprint first

Fingerprinting is now used all the time to solve lots of crimes – but when was it first used?

a) USA, 1921

b) Argentina, 1892

c) London, 1856

Answer:

b) Francesca Rojas admitted murdering her two children after her fingerprints were found in blood on the door of her home. The children had been beaten to death and the police at first suspected a male friend of Rojas. (She had accused him herself.) Then they found her fingerprint and she owned up.

> I HAVE A BOYFRIEND WHO SAID HE WOULD MARRY ME SO LONG AS THE CHILDREN DID NOT COME WITH ME. NO ONE WOULD HAVE THEM SO...

Nowadays parents who want to get rid of kids just buy them a computer with a load of games. They never see them again.

Fingerprint facts

Here are a few fascinating fingerprint facts:

- Fingerprints last for life ... or even longer! Egyptian mummies have fingerprints and they are 3,000 years old!
- If the tips are burned or rubbed off the same pattern will grow back. The American gangster, John Dillinger, paid doctors in 1934 to perform plastic surgery on his finger tips. They failed. Friends suggested he dip the fingers in acid. This worked for a while but by the time he was caught the patterns had reappeared. Another gangster, Robert Pitts, had skin transplanted from his chest to his fingertips. This got rid of the fingerprints but he was convicted on other evidence ... and the doctor who operated on his fingers went to jail too!
- The Ancient Chinese knew about identifying people by their fingerprints. They used a thumbprint in wax as a 'signature' that couldn't be forged.
- In a smash-and-grab raid in Zurich, Switzerland in 1970 the thief's finger was sliced off by the breaking glass. The police matched the fingertip with the fingerprints they had on file and caught him.

GREAT FIND! YOU KNOW WHAT THIS MEANS, CONSTABLE?

HE'LL NEVER PICK HIS NOSE AGAIN?

TERRIBLE 20TH CENTURY

The 20th century saw *lots* of new inventions – and lots of new crimes. Once you invent cars, you've got speeding, and dangerous driving and ram-raiding…

Invent aeroplanes and by 1947 you have the first hijacker. Invent computers and you have 'hackers', stealing everything from money to secrets. There's no doubt about it, the 20th century was another prime crime time.

Laugh with your local lawman

Do you have a friendly local policeman who visits your school? You know the sort…

These popular plods like nothing better than interested young people who ask them questions. So here are a few simple questions on crime to try on them. To make it more fun, we suggest you handcuff them to a desk and release them only if they get more than five simple questions right.

1 Car theft (England, 1976) Two car thieves stole a car but were caught when they tried to sell it. Who did they try to sell it to?
a) A policeman who had just heard the car reported stolen.
b) The owner of the car.
c) A car thief who drove it off without paying.

2 Detection (England, 1951) A horse called Lady Wonder showed police where a murder victim was buried. How did Lady Wonder do this?

a) Lady Wonder pawed at the grave with her hoof and uncovered a leg.
b) Lady Wonder dialled 999 and phoned the police (or she may have dialled Neigh! Neigh! Neigh!).
c) Lady Wonder tapped out the name of the place on a typewriter.

3 Fraud (USA, 1977) A man was bumped by a car in the street. A passer-by said, 'Lie down in the road, pretend to be hurt, and claim a fortune from the driver.' What happened?
a) The driver wasn't insured so the fake victim got nothing.
b) The driver panicked and gave the victim a million dollars he had in his briefcase.
c) When the fake victim lay down in the road the car rolled over him and crushed him to death.

4 Prohibition (USA, 1929) It was against the law to have alcohol in the USA. A woman was shot dead by a law officer for having alcohol – even though she didn't *actually* have any. What made the officer think she was guilty?

a) He thought he smelled alcohol in the room.
b) She offered him a glass of apple juice and said, 'Have a whiskey,' as a joke.
c) He was drunk at the time.

5 Kidnapping (Italy, 1973) Kidnappers took the grandson of J Paul Getty and demanded $17 million. Getty had BILLIONS but refused to pay. The kidnappers finally got him to pay by sending him what?
a) A tape of the grandson begging grandad to pay up.
b) His grandson's teddy-bear with its throat cut.
c) His grandson's ear.

6 Assassination (Russia, 1934) Sergei Kirov, the leader of the people of the city of Leningrad, was assassinated. Who did it?
a) His boss, Joseph Stalin, leader of Russia (because Kirov was too popular).
b) His assistant, Yuri Topov (because he wanted Kirov's job).
c) His wife, Olga Kirov (because she thought it would be quicker than a divorce).

7 Punishment (Britain, 1965) Britain banned execution for nearly every crime. But you could still be executed for treason, and for what else?
a) Making your own ten-pound notes.
b) Insulting the queen.
c) Being a violent pirate.

8 Robbery (USA, 1970s) A bank robber disguised himself by putting a pillowcase over his head. He failed. Why?
a) He forgot to cut eye-holes in the pillowcase.
b) The pillowcase had his name on it.
c) The pillowcase was dusty and he sneezed it off.

9 Con trick (USA, 1916) A banker called Yoakum paid Professor Erlicht $100,000 for an envelope and a bucket of water. What did Yoakum think they could do?
a) Make you live for ever.
b) Run a car engine.
c) Poison his wife without leaving a trace.

10 Murder (France, 1869) A tailor called Voirbo killed an old miser then hid the body down a well. Many months later a clever detective, Gustave Mace, found a clue that showed the miser had died in Voirbo's room. What?

a) He looked under the settee and found the miser's purse.

b) He looked under the stone floor and found the miser's blood.

c) He looked under the kitchen sink and found the miser's washing-up cloth.

Answers:

1b) It's bad luck. Of all the people to meet they had to meet the man whose car they'd stolen. They were nearly as unlucky as the San Fernando bank robber who dashed into the street with a fortune – and was knocked down by his getaway car.

2c) Lady Wonder used her nose to tap messages on a typewriter. Her owner claimed the horse got messages from the spirit world. Spooky or what?

3c) Which just goes to show, cheats never beats.

4a) The officer thought he smelled alcohol so he shot the woman and beat her husband to the ground with his pistol. There's a policeman who takes his job seriously. A Chicago mother of ten was given life in prison the same year. Her crime? She had hidden a bottle of gin.

5c) They hinted they'd send his grandson back to him one piece at a time. Grandad finally paid just $2 million and got the rest of his grandson back. What must he have thought when he opened the body-part parcel?

6a) Stalin couldn't stand the competition. No one was allowed to be more popular than him. He had everyone killed who stood in his way. From 1934 to 1938 at least seven million people 'disappeared' in Stalin's murder spree. He always claimed, of course, that they were criminals and that their deaths were their rightful punishment. Some of the trials were a joke, though. An awful lot of crime – a terrible total of punishments.

7c) No one since 1965 has ever been executed for being a violent pirate. This is just as well because the British government would have a job finding someone to do the execution. The last hangman died years ago. Maybe they could get some tips from the USA where they still kill people with electric chairs, poison injections and hanging.

8a) It's hard to believe anyone could be that daft. He was. As daft as the bank robber who actually got out of the bank with the loot and waved for a taxi. But the light on top of the car wasn't a taxi sign – it was a sign that said, 'Police'. Oooops!

9b) 'Professor' Erlicht told Yoakum he had a special mixture that with water would run a car – no more need to drill for oil or pay for petrol, you could make fuel for a penny a litre. Erlicht put the secret in an envelope and sold the sealed envelope to Yoakum for $100,000. He also gave Yoakum a bucket of water and they tested the mixture on a car. It worked! There *is* a mixture that will let water run a car – but it costs far, far more than petrol to make – and it wrecks the car engine after a couple of hundred miles. But Erlicht got away with the money.

10b) The body was found when the water in the well turned foul from the rotting corpse. But that was months after the miser had disappeared. Voirbo seemed to have got away with murder. The killer's room had been scrubbed clean. But detective Mace had the floor dug up and looked UNDER the stones. That was the blood that Voirbo couldn't clean. That was the clue that sent vicious Voirbo to the guillotine.

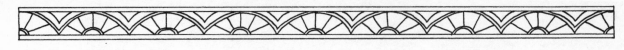

 My mum

SUFFERING SCHOOLS

Children have probably been beaten since the first cave-kid trod on his dad's big toe. Parents punish kids in all sorts of ways for all sorts of 'crimes'. But once the child gets to school they find that a) the 'laws' are written down and called 'School Rules' and b) the punishments can be really rotten. Still, at least in the 21st century it's not as painful for pupils as it was in the punishing past.

Cane that kid

In 2001, a Liverpool school said it wanted to start smacking bad children again. That had been banned in British schools in 1987 but the Headmaster From Hell argued that the Bible said it was a good idea and 40 other public schools in Britain backed him. The brutal Bible says…

> Punish the child with the rod and save his soul from death.
> A child's heart is full of stupidity, but the rod will drive it out of him.
> A father who doesn't beat his son hates him; the father who loves his son is careful to discipline him.

But there is another bit of the Bible that says…

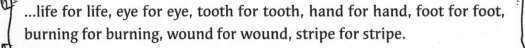
> …life for life, eye for eye, tooth for tooth, hand for hand, foot for foot, burning for burning, wound for wound, stripe for stripe.

What about that then, horrible Headmaster? If you believe in the Bible then any teacher who smacks a child has to be smacked back!

PLEASE, SIR, IF YOU DON'T MIND I'LL LET MY BIG BROTHER SMACK YOU BACK!

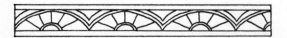 

Gruesome guide

Schools have rules for pupils – but there are rules for teachers too. This one's from a British school in the 1930s…

And there were some rules that teachers probably didn't need to be told…

Hurting someone like this is called 'corporal punishment'. Since it has been banned, these 'corporal punishment' rules for teachers are now historical documents – and some are horrible historical documents. This one is from a 20th-century boys' school…

Corporal Punishment – Teachers' Notes

GENERAL NOTES

Corporal punishment at this school is for serious offences. It is given with a cane upon the clothed seat of the offender. Corporal punishment is never to be given to any other part of the body and a standard school cane must always be used.

CANING OFFENCES

The following are caning offences which will always earn corporal punishment: BULLYING; SMOKING; VANDALISM; HOOLIGANISM; SWEARING; THEFT; LATE-COMING; TRUANCY; WILFUL LAZINESS; SERIOUS MISCONDUCT OF ANY KIND.

PUNISHMENT CANES

Housemasters in the Junior School have a standard junior punishment cane. Housemasters in the Senior School (with boys aged 15 and upwards) may use a slightly longer and thicker senior punishment cane.

PUNISHMENT REPORT

A boy sentenced to the cane is placed on Punishment Report. He will be issued with a Punishment Report Card which he must take home to be signed by his parents before the caning is given.

THE CANING

Punishment parades are always held after afternoon registration. The punishment cane should be laid out on the desk together with the official punishment book, and a suitable chair provided for bending over. Boys are never caned in the 'touching toes' position, which is impractical and may even be somewhat dangerous.

The boy should come into the study, hand the master his Punishment Report Card and then stand at attention to await further instructions. The master should study the card and explain to the offender exactly why he is getting the cane. Position him over the chair and before starting the punishment, check that no padding or extra pairs of underpants have been brought in to lessen the pain.

HOW MANY STROKES?

The minimum punishment is two strokes, with three as the average for first-timers. Repeated bad behaviour may earn six of the best whilst the most allowed under school regulations is nine strokes.

Lay the cane on firmly, or else there is little point doing it. The aim is to put the fear of the cane into the boy. Schoolboys will not respect a master who pussyfoots where the cane is concerned: do the job properly. Do not spare the rod, even with a new boy. The punishment is for his own good.

THE PUNISHMENT BOOK

After the caning, the boy must sign the punishment book. Tell the boy that you have no wish to see his name in the book again and send him off to his lessons, asking him to send in the next boy if any are still waiting.

The teachers were also told that telling the parents was all part of the punishment. But sometimes the parents were on the side of their boys…

Try that teacher

In 1922 a newspaper in Newport, Shropshire, reported a case where a father had a headmaster and two teachers charged by the police for beating his son.

⤜ The Newport News ⤝
HEAD CASE

Mr Walter Brook, headmaster of Newport Grammar School, and two senior teachers were today charged with assault for the caning they gave to Frank Wright.

Frank Wright was seen smoking in the street and reported. The boy said he did not know it was against the school rules. The next morning the boy was called in to see the headmaster who said he was going to make an example of him. The beating in front of the rest of the school was severe.

Frank Wright's father called to see the headmaster and said that he allowed his son to smoke. He

FRANK WRIGHT (OR WRONG?)

asked to see the school rule that banned smoking outside school hours. The headmaster told him that there was no printed rule. Mr Wright reported the matter to the police and today the teachers appeared in court.

The magistrates heard the evidence and gave their decision.

But what was the magistrates' decision?
a) The teachers were set free.
b) The teachers were locked in prison.
c) The teachers were caned.

Answer:

a) Not only were the teachers set free, but the magistrate said:

This case should not have been brought. The headmaster was quite right to cane the boy.

Frank Wright had not wanted to be caned and he had struggled while two teachers held him down. After the beating he lay on the floor and wept. So the magistrate added: 'It is a pity young Wright didn't take it like a man.'

Sometimes it's hard being a boy. The case went to a higher court, but this judge just said…

Both the boy AND his father deserved to be punished!

So now you know. The boy suffered because a) his father was to blame and b) he was a wimp. The teachers were not to blame at all. That's all right then.

Pain in the grass

Many pupils remember their canings fifty or more years later. Some always remember their first caning – especially if it was for a little crime.

My first 'swishing' came in my second term at school. My crime was using the lawn in front of the main school building as a short cut when I was late for a lesson. I knew it was against the rules. That lawn was the first sight visitors saw and if all boys were to ignore the rule the fine green lawn would soon have turned into a muddy field.

At least that boy understood *why* he was being punished.

Brutal birch

Some people still believe the best way to stop crime is to…

BRING BACK THE BIRCH!

No, he isn't asking us all to plant a tree in our back garden. He is suggesting we take the twigs from a birch tree, tie them into a bundle and use them to whip young criminals on the bare backside.

This charming punishment was stopped in the 1940s in Britain but went on for another 20 years in the Isle of Man.

MAN'S GOT TO DO WHAT MAN'S GOT TO DO!

The birch was supposed to be a good cure for young criminals – so when you left school at 14 and escaped the cane, you faced the birch instead. There were even books telling policemen and prison officers how to birch someone, like this one from 1938…

- The punishment is usually given in a cell or private room, either near the court or at a nearby police station. The birch is applied across the buttocks, on the bare flesh.
- The most common method is to bend the boy over a low bench or table. His hands, and sometimes his feet, may be held by helpers.
- In some cases a man takes the boy on his back, drawing the boy's hands over his shoulders; another constable holds the boy's feet, drawing his legs around the sides of the first man; the first constable then leans forward, and the birch is applied by a third.
- In some cases the boy is bent over and his head held between a man's knees, whilst a second administers the birch.

- In one district the boy is strapped to a triangle.
- In Scotland the boy is usually laid flat on a form (a long bench), two police officers sitting astride the form at each end, one holding his elbows and the other his feet, while a third gives the birching.

That was the plan. So what actually happened at a birching? Well, this is how a witness described the beating of a young thief in 1887...

The officer who held the birch stepped forward and with all his might started the punishment. The boy began the most pitiful howling and yelling and red marks appeared almost immediately across his buttocks. After three strokes his right buttock was like a piece of raw beef. After the sixth stroke the constable moved round to the other side of the form and administered six hefty strokes across the left buttock. The boy gave the most unearthly yells and blood was soon showing. The constable was proud of the fact that the criminal would not be able to sit down for quite a time.

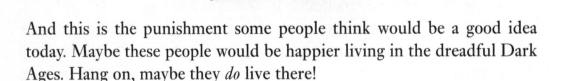

And this is the punishment some people think would be a good idea today. Maybe these people would be happier living in the dreadful Dark Ages. Hang on, maybe they *do* live there!

EPILOGUE

So, you've discovered that crimes and punishments can be horribly cruel – and awfully odd. Here are some of the craziest crimes and the pottiest punishments in history. Before you finish this book, you can decide which are top of the top-tens for yourself...

Top ten crazy crimes

At the time, these were signs of the rebelling Scots, of course. King George's soldiers were allowed to shoot a man in tartan on the spot. A Scots piper was hanged in York for playing the bagpipes – the judge said they were 'an instrument of war'.

After ten at night, husbands may have been drunk and they shouldn't beat a woman if they were drunk.

Clearly Athens wanted to show the tourists how smart the city was.

Those men should be fishing or mending nets. Plenty of time for knitting on the cold winter nights.

A comb could be used as a weapon. This law came after a 13-year-old boy was killed when he was stabbed with a sharpened steel comb.

In the early days of the town, the owner of the bar had a pet moose that he used to get drunk. The moose would then stumble around the town causing chaos. The only way the law-makers could stop it was to pass a law so the moose could not cross the pavement and get into the bar.

As Oklahoma is hundreds of miles from the sea, no one *ever* broke this law.

The law bans the sale of dolls that do not have human faces. It probably has something to do with the old witchcraft laws.

In case you were a busker trying to beg for money as you sing.

King Charles II wanted England to become rich from selling lots of wool. So he passed a law saying that even dead people had to use it.

Top ten potty and painful punishments

1 If an English lord was sentenced to hang he could ask to have the hanging rope made out of silk so his throat wouldn't be scratched. Stretched – but not scratched.

2 In Afghanistan, in the 1990s, it was against the law for anyone to fly a kite. The punishment was a hard whipping.

3 A 1845 British law says it is illegal to commit suicide. Anyone caught attempting to kill themselves would be hanged!

4 Vlad the Impaler welcomed two Italian lords to his court. They refused to take off their hats to show their respect. Their punishment was having their hats nailed to their heads.

5 Even libraries have laws – if your book is late back you pay a fine. A book was borrowed in a US library in 1823 and returned in 1968. The fine was $22,000.

6 King Gustav III of Sweden was sure that coffee was a poison. To prove it he sentenced a murderer to death by drinking coffee every day. And to show he was right the King ordered another murderer to drink tea every day. Two doctors were given the task of checking the experiment. The doctors died first. The King was murdered in 1792. The tea drinker died many years later at the age of 83, and the coffee drinker lived longest of all!

7 Anyone who was a drunken nuisance in the 17th or 18th centuries could be placed in 'The Drunkard's Cloak' i.e. driven up and down the streets wearing nothing but a barrel.

8 Robert Daumiens is sentenced to be torn into quarters by horses in 1757. His crime? He'd plotted to kill the French king.

9 Saint Catherine was sentenced to death in the 4th century for being a Christian. The method of execution was to be tied to a spiked wheel and rolled down a hill. We remember this today with the firework which is still called a Catherine wheel.

10 Tamerlane the Great ruled Samarkand from 1336 to 1405 and he loved a good joke. But if anyone told him one he'd heard before he would have them executed. What a great idea!

NOW WHY NOT VISIT WWW.terry-deary.COM?